BRITISH
RAILWAYS
ILLUSTRATED

SUMMER SPECIAL No.13

ILLUSTRATED

SUMMER SPECIAL No.13

All New Photographs and Articles!

Front Cover. The final Merchant Navy Pacific, 35030 ELDER DEMPSTER LINES, at Eastleigh shed, during its years as a Weymouth (70G) engine, 1964-1967. Photograph The Transport Treasury.

Rear Cover. As inviting a prospect as this book itself... Photograph The Transport Treasury.

Frontispiece. The shadows lengthen at Nine Elms, 1967. Photograph Paul Hocquard, The Transport Treasury.

You'll Remember those Black and White Days...

IRWELL PRESS CO UK E-mail George@Irwellpress.co.uk

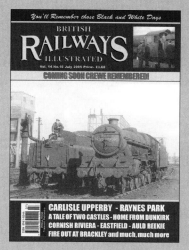

EDITORIAL MATTERS
Contributions, submissions, photographs or whatever (remember the contributor must address and attend to copyright), readers' letters, bouquets and brickbats for **British Railways Illustrated** must be addressed to Editor,

Chris Hawkins
at 59A, High Street, Clophill, Bedfordshire MK45 4BE
E-mail chris@irwellpress.co.uk
Tel.01525 861888 or
Fax. 01525 862044
Printed & Bound by Amadeus Press, Bradford
Copyright :- Irwell Press Ltd. 2005

Aspects of Water Troughs

Colin Bennett, with some follow-up points from BRILL in 1999

It may be useful to remind ourselves of what might seem the obvious: 'In order that long non-stop runs can be successfully carried out on the railways it is necessary, where non-condensing simple steam locomotives are used for this purpose, that an adequate supply of fuel and water is carried on the tender attached to the engine.' (George Wooliscroft, an LMS Engineer, in an account for the interested layman in *The LMS Magazine* called, simply, *Water Troughs for Locomotives;* see also my ramblings in *British Railways Illustrated,* March and May 1999.)

There were few runs in Britain that tested the coal capacity of any tender (though some were close, needing last-minute top ups, 'a little bit extra' on the footplate and so on). It was water, a continuous supply of it, that was the obvious problem. Now no tender could carry all the water necessary for a decent run and with a thousand gallons of water equivalent to an extra carriage it early on in Britain became obvious that replenishing the tender en route was an answer. Water troughs were expensive to build and needed maintenance but the burden could

be eased by siting them where supplies were cheap or of good quality – or preferably both. These benefits were often counterbalanced by the costs of machinery and its upkeep.

By the time of the Grouping a sophisticated system of troughs had been in operation and typical expresses of 300 tons headed as often as not by 4-4-0s were using about 3,000 gallons every 100 miles. This made for a convenient spacing between water troughs, or at least between the main stops where engines were changed or took water.

Fairly obviously the first consideration was straight(ish) and level line for a sufficient distance but there were more complications than you'd think and for some 60 yards at each end of the troughs a slight gradient was set up, 1 in 360. This provided a dip coming into the troughs and a rise at the end. At each end of the trough it tapered up to terminate as a flat plate. This was to prevent the water pick-up scoop striking the trough if lowered early or if it were not raised quickly enough. A considerable clearance was allowed for in either case. Troughs were praced between the

rails, and would characteristically be about 16 inches wide and 6 inches deep, made up of pressed sheet steel, riveted together. In the early years the troughing was fixed to longitudinal timbers but they were later held by a variety of metal trusses, lugs and so on, so that the top of the trough was something like 2½ inches above rail level and the level of the water about 1½ inches above rail level. The proportions varied from company to company; it might be thought that these dimensions were more or less arbitrary but they weren't.

As early as the turn of the century exhaustive tests proved that dimensions should be critical. In extensive trials the Pennsylvania Railroad in the USA (where tenders were bigger and scoops might have been too, though they were of course limited by the same gauge as in Britain) found that at 40mph (regarded as the most economical scooping speed) 75% more water was wasted with a 29 inch trough than one 19 inches wide. In fact, the narrower the trough the less water was wasted at all speeds. About the same time the New York Railroad found that in double heading, the

Left and below. A typical Midland installation, at Melton Mowbray, a 50,000 gallon tank for each trough. These are in the fast lines, with up and down loops to the sides intended mainly to hold the endless freights while the passenger trains swept through. The line became double track at Brentingby box, the other side of the bridge from which the pictures were taken. In fact, though officially termed Melton, many local crews habitually called them Brentingby troughs. First, on 18 July 1958, is a typical Midland line train of the time, a Black Five (unidentified) headed by a 2P 4-4-0, 40690. There were poor returns for the second engine on water troughs if both 'scooped' at the same time and crews had a standing arrangement that the second one would draw first, easing up the scoop towards the middle of the trough as the leading engine lowered its own scoop. The Type 2 D7520 is on the up loop, waiting the signal to proceed, on 15 August 1966. The troughs by this time are 'dry' and no longer in use. The second man looks out mournfully at the soon to disappear scene. Photographs Peter Groom.

second engine took only 25% of the water scooped by the pilot in the lead. Enginemen both there (the US) and 'over here' had fallen into an informal arrangement of taking water in turn, getting half the trough each as it were. The NYR found that a narrower but longer trough, 19 inches wide, was much more economical, in that much less water was wasted. According to *The Railway Gazette*, The Midland Railway at this period used troughs 17¾ inches wide with scoops only 10 inches wide. This was said to give 'most excellent' results while the Great Western troughs, 'owing to their design, give a minimum of waste'. Just as in locomotive draughting, the companies all had their own set of variables, ones which, whatever their relative efficiencies, 'worked for them'.

Many sets of troughs had two tanks, with a capacity somewhere in the region of 50,000 gallons, one for each trough. Yet this obviously varied. Some sets seem to have had only one tank, while installations such as Bushey on the LNW with four troughs certainly did not have four tanks. It was after all, merely a question of plumbing.

The vital thing was to fill the trough quickly after the passage of a train. How this was achieved

varied in detail of course from company to company and obviously new developments were made over the years. Big piping, big as possible, was essential with the water supplied through levelling valves. Water was best fed towards either end of a trough, longitudinally down its length, avoiding losses by splash over the side. Waste could be serious, for at many sites water had to obtained by wells, pumping and so on and was therefore not cheap. However easily the water was won in the first place, softening it was an expensive process and as early as 1933 the LMS authorised a block grant of £9,500 (an enormous sum then) for the 'recovery of softened spilled water where water softening plants have been installed, and which at present drain to waste'. How this was to be done remained unstated but the troughs involved were: Moore, Whitmore, Hademore, Newbold, Bushey, Melton Mowbray, Loughborough and Oakley.

In 1919 the most advanced system of the time opened at Oakley on the Great Northern, where previously no means existed of taking on water in the 80 miles between London and Werrington, north of Peterborough. Oakley had troughs that filled in just 2½ minutes, an efficiency that hardly

LONDON MIDLAND & SCOTTISH RAILWAY COMPANY.

MECHANICAL & ELECTRICAL ENGINEERING COMMITTEE.

Euston Station, N.W.1.

27th April, 1932.

Present :-

    Charles Booth, Esq., in the Chair,

    W. L. Hichens, Esq.

    J. W. Murray, Esq.

    A. E. Pullar, Esq.

    G.R.T. Taylor, Esq.

    Sir Thomas Williams.

Attended By :- Sir Harold Hartley, Mr. W. A. Stanier, Mr. F.A.C. Leigh and Mr. J. Shearman.

S.T.Jones - Secretary

Report on Water Troughs and Water Capacity of Tenders.

        Read the following report (5th April 1932) from the Chief Mechanical Engineer :-

        "In connection with the interchange of engines from one Division to another, it has been found that the smaller capacity tenders in general use on L.& N.W. engines have not sufficient capacity to carry between the troughs on the Midland Division where the spacings were roughly 50 miles against 30 on the Western Division, and it was decided to investigate the whole matter and come to a decision as to the most economical capacity for tenders and spacing of troughs, both for present and future requirements.

        "The water capacity of the tenders in general use on the Western Division engines was 3,000 gallons, whilst those in use on the Midland are generally 3,500 gallons capacity.

        "The investigation which has been made shews that the principal costs involved are :-

(1) Maintenance and capital charges on tenders.
(2) Cost of hauling the tender.

        "Both these items increase as the size of the tender increases.

(3) Maintenance and capital charges on troughs.
(4) Total annual cost of water.

        "These items decrease as the size of the tender increases, No.3 because the number of troughs is reduced and No.4 because less water is wasted if water be taken from a column than if it is picked up from troughs.

"It may be mentioned here that a deflector plate has recently been introduced and this is being fitted to all new tenders as they are built, and as regards existing tenders the question is being examined with a view to ascertaining how far it would be an economical proposition to apply these to existing tenders.

"The combined effect of the four items listed above has been embodied in a curve which is given on diagram 2.* This curve is a hypothetical one, and was prepared for passenger service only, taking the line from Euston to Crewe as an example, and assuming that 120 engines were necessary to work the non-stop trains. The number of troughs varies from five for the smallest tenders to none for the largest.

"It will be seen that the cost does not vary much in relation to tender capacity until it becomes necessary to change from six to eight wheels to carry the greater weight of water. The best capacity for any given route depends very much on local conditions, but our experience has so far shewn that 3,500 gallons capacity is the best for all general purposes. However, it may be that if longer non-stop runs are called for on heavy freight trains, or larger engines are developed in the future, some increase on the 3,500 gallon capacity may be necessary.

"The curve indicates clearly that if tender capacities in excess of 4,000 gallons are required, then it will probably be cheaper to lay down extra troughs rather than build larger capacity tenders.

"(Signed) W.A. Stanier".

Noted.

*Unfortunately now long lost. The railway companies had an annoying habit of rarely including diagrams and plans in their Minutes.

seems to have been bettered throughout the rest of the century. Each trough had a substantial levelling valve which opened immediately the water dropped by half an inch, closing at once as soon as the level returned to full.

Troughs were industrial installations in their own right; apart from the machinery which had to be housed, there were pumps and pump houses (Oakley had a 100ft well lined in cast iron and used refurbished locomotive boilers to bring up the water!), tanks, pipes and specialised permanent way. The 100,000 gallon tank at Oakley was six hundred yards from the well and its pump house.

From the 1930s, as mentioned above, a good number of troughs got water softeners too, so though much of the operation was automatic, these things didn't just sit there; they were constantly inspected, maintained and serviced, with full time staff required, say, in the case of Oakley's boilers. Oddly, Oakley had troughs made of timber not sheet steel and it may have been the last one so equipped. Seasons and weather played a part in the maintenance of troughs; I've never seen it recorded but the wrong kind of leaves and sundry debris (dead pheasants, unfortunate lavatory material) would need removal. Whenever there was a hint of frost

men had to be in constant attendance to break up the ice. Nice job... In upland districts troughs were sometimes equipped with a system of steam pipes fed from a boiler, in order to stop them freezing solid but in latter years BR seems to have relied on the constant movement of the water; even if freezing did begin, a scoop would soon disrupt it again. You hoped.

Of all the trackside features, perhaps troughs are the most missed – except, maybe, by the blokes charged with maintaining them!

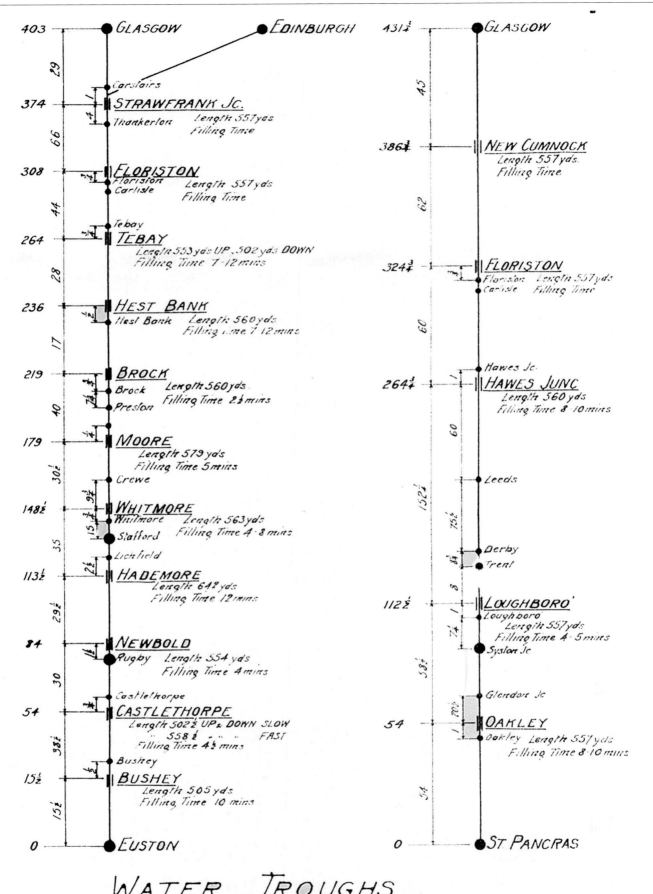

WATER TROUGHS
LONDON TO GLASGOW & EDINBURGH

Above. Down on the deck. Back at Bushey, illustrated in such detail in *British Railways Illustrated,* March and May 1999, with 8F 48325 of Willesden on the Down Slow with coal empties in March 1963. It can only be assumed that the photographer knew nothing of the danger he was in. Apart from slipping on the slimy baulks in the roaring din of the trains you could be flattened by a mass of water travelling at 40mph or an errant lump of coal. Photograph J.G. Walmsley, The Transport Treasury.

Left. A Bletchley 8F, 48656, lumbers along the Up Slow at Bushey with coal for the capital, 16 March 1963. Some odd sections of troughing lie at the side, discarded after some replacement/repair work. Photograph J.G. Walmsley, The Transport Treasury.

AWS fitted 8F 2-8-0 48759 on the Up Slow, March 1963. The troughs were littered with debris at this time but historically the care of them had been much more particular but look at Bushey in the final picture – it seems to have always been in a state! The end was in sight for Bushey of course by this time and 'the wires' were making their remorseless way south. By this time it was inevitable that any attention would only be the minimum required to keep the troughs going. Bushey held an odd significance. The troughs were only there really so that engines could fill up before reaching Euston; there were no water columns there and tenders had to be sufficiently full for both a long wait and the run back to Camden. By 1963 there were far fewer locos working into the terminus but those that did (since 1961 in fact) faced the even longer trip back to Willesden. For freights also, Bushey was something of a last 'top-up', for the journey on to the London yards could be a protracted one. Photograph J.G. Walmsley, The Transport Treasury.

Above. With what looks like the 'Royal Scot', one of the by-now nearly ubiquitous EE Type 4s, D383, takes water on the Down Fast at Bushey in March 1963. The Fireman is looking back no doubt in some concern at the overflow – the early BR diesel boilers were temperamental at the best of times... An EMU (later Class 501) is on the Up third rail line – the Bakerloo Line/Watford Electric DC tracks ran on the west side. Photograph J.G. Walmsley, The Transport Treasury.

Below. We move on to 1964 at Bushey and the wires have arrived, the top lamp iron moving down to the smokebox door and the middle lower one moving over in the meantime. The 8F with the coal train on the Up Slow is Willesden's 48541; there were pipes everywhere in the vicinity of troughs of course and some sort of renewal work would be indicated by the length of pipe abandoned here. From earlier photographs in BRILL in 1999 this particular piece would seem to have been here for at least

a year! To repeat some points from those articles, the troughs were fed from a borehole in the Chilterns, carried in a twelve inch cast iron main all the way on to Willesden and Camden: *When the troughs were closed down and removed it was decided to dig up the pipe, though the shortcomings of the available plans led to some slightly farcical outcomes. At Willesden, all the cocks were turned off and the assault on the main begun. It was some time before the relevant stopcock was uncovered and the resulting geyser poured out enough water to flood the up slow for three or four days. At Bushey, the plans indicated that the main ran along the down fast but on digging it up no sign of the pipe could be found. One of the 'old boys' was summoned up and by a mixture of divining and folk memory, he was able to indicate its true position, under the Down Slow.* That's the extra arch in the bridge over Oxhey Road, made when the LNW instituted the electric service just before the First World War.

Double headed water taking in progress – one of the late great E.D. Bruton's excellent descriptions follows: 'As the tender tank of the train engine begins to overflow, the pilot is now getting its fill in turn, as they traverse Hest Bank troughs at 60 mph at 5.12pm on Saturday May 24th 1952. They are heading south with the 1.30pm Glasgow Central-London Euston 'Mid Day Scot'. Stanier Black Five 4-6-0 44708 is piloting rebuilt Royal Scot 46118 ROYAL WELCH FUSILIER with at least sixteen on. All but three are in carmine and cream livery.' Photograph E.D. Bruton.

A notable overflow from Caprotti Class 5 44752 with the northbound 'Pines Express' on Whitmore, 4 September 1959. At this earlier period the look of the troughs is almost manicured – the scruffy look of Bushey towards the end was owed to the neglect endemic at the fag-end of steam working. Photograph Ray Farrell.

All smoke and shade as 4F 0-6-0 4323 with an excursion takes water on former L&Y Luddendenfoot troughs in the 1930s. Photograph Locofotos.

The view ahead – this is Rowington troughs (which seems to have been the alternative name for Hatton) from a DMU in 1962. Like other GWR troughs there is no special planking, paving or whatever. The Great Western troughs, 'owing to their design' (gave) 'a minimum of waste' claimed *The Railway Gazette*. Planking and paving was to protect the ballast from wash – presumably the *Gazette* was right, and ballast on GW troughs 'owing to their design' did not need protecting.

Poor old scruffy 46126 ROYAL ARMY SERVICE CORPS sets up a deluge passing along Whitmore troughs under the new wires, 15 June 1962. It does not need much calculation, from these pictures and others in the 1999 BRILLs, that literally tons of water could be thrown off while an engine took water, especially if the Fireman was struggling to wind up the scoop. At sixty miles an hour, or even much less, this of course could be fatal to anyone unwise enough to be in the way. We have be thankful for the ignorance of various photographers, unaware they might lay down their lives in the cause of future railway nostalgia. PW men hated troughs (making the close scenes at Hatton in BRILL June 2005 with men posed by a passing train quite inexplicable) and made themselves scarce. It was common to post extra lookouts, such were the risks. Photographs Ray Farrell.

Whitmore on 4 September 1959 with 8F 48767 on a southbound goods. Photograph Ray Farrell.

Another of E.D. Bruton's fine portraits – and another of his detailed descriptions: 'Kettering 8F, 48645 off its regular route, enters Bushey troughs with down Class 'K' empty mineral wagons at 9.16am BST on June 30th 1951 at about 20 mph. The pick-up scoop is just engaging the water. The stock is a mixed bag of old wooden ex-PO wagons and some MWT/MOT steel bodied ones. The train is on the Down Slow. The loco was Southern built at Brighton Works in 1943 (batch 8625-8249).' The unpalatable fact is that, inevitably, along with other debris, lavatory waste found its way into troughs on occasion and, equally inevitably, into locomotive tenders. Still, you needed to be philosophical about it: "Just as well the Restaurant Cars didn't pick up from the troughs, then" retorts one BR stalwart frequently encountered elsewhere in these vaunted columns.

Factory Junction Fourum

R.C. Riley again, on the lookout for the more venerable Southern classes, at Factory Junction, Battersea, on 23 August 1958. Summer Saturdays were always more likely to bring out the 4-4-0s, E1s, Ls and so on, on passenger work, along with ageing Arthurs; the unexpected was 'in the air' as it were. In the meantime one had to be content with mere Pacifics... A short walk from Stewarts Lane shed, armed with a trackside pass, brought one to this elevated spot, dominated by Battersea power station. The 'Factory' of the name (carried also on the box) was the old LCD works. On the left-hand page we have (top) 34092 CITY OF WELLS on a down boat express and (below) 34085 501 SQUADRON with

the down Golden Arrow. Right (top) 34013 OKEHAMPTON passes with an up Margate-Derby Friargate train and right (below) is another light Pacific in original condition, a scruffy 34100 APPLEDORE with another down boat working. The Derby working was an interesting one – a B1 would be waiting at Kensington to take over for the onward run to Derby, over the Great Central. More of Factory Junction in a future issue of BRILL... All photographs R.C. Riley, The Transport Treasury.

With the driver apparently distracted (the Report records a 'failure to control the train') the 21.35 Penzance-Paddington (1A07) behind 50041 BULWARK came to grief on the station approaches, in the fashion so chillingly recorded here. There were no fatalities, thank goodness, which is an indication of how robust the stock of the period had become. The point to contemplate is, *it could have been so much worse.* Imagine if the train had had a straight run (i.e., not put through the speed restricted crossover which derailed it) right into the heart of the station. It would have gone across 'The Lawn' and ended up in the Refreshment Room or down the Circle Line subway. The ensuing disaster would still be recalled today with a shudder instead of being largely and, mercifully, forgotten.

Thanks to Alec Swain and Mike Romans.

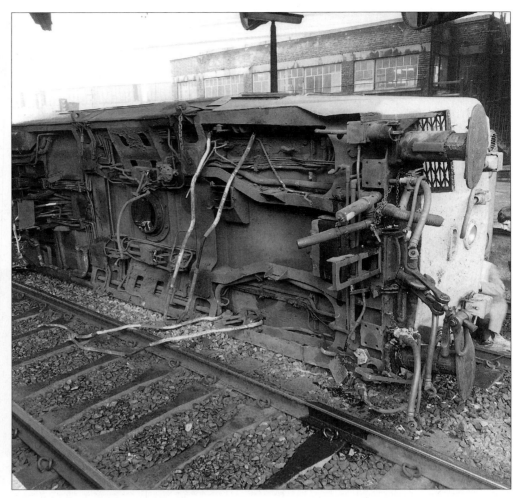

The photographs are presented from east (the loco end) to west, in order of taking. The first, here, shows 50041 (No.2 end, leading) lying between No.7 and No.8 platforms.

Paddington, Tuesday 23 November 1983

The stricken BULWARK – this time No.1 end. The locomotive was moving into the station left (west) to right (east).

The loco was 'shepherded' in as it were by the platform edging and thankfully speed was such that the sliding bulk could not 'jump' the platform.

The damage to the coping stones shows where the loco dropped on to its side and lost its bogies – the rear bogie stayed there, the front bogie ran on for a while (with or without the loco) to come to rest alongside it. It must have presented a truly appalling sight from the old Arrival signal box.

Leading vehicle BG 92039 on its side followed by BG 84578 leaning at five degrees towards the north side. Paddington Goods Shed stands beyond, by then the property of National Carriers (NCL).

Sleeping car 10563 at rest with BG 84512.

Above. Wider view of the stricken train; the sleeping cars 10563 (nearest camera) and 10561 are seen to form a 'V' around BG 84512.

Left. Looking east into Paddington; note the BRUFF road/rail vehicle with re-railing equipment on the right. Paddington Goods has long been demolished and redeveloped. The only change to come out of the incident concerned the speed differentials, which were then included in the 'Morpeth' signalling. At the time of the accident they were such that there were no permanent AWS magnet warnings running into Paddington.

Summer Saturday at Surbiton 1st August 1964

By Alistair Nisbet

Traffic on the main lines out of Waterloo on summer Saturdays in the 1950s and 1960s was for the whole of the morning and much of the afternoon every bit as heavy as during the weekday peak hour of 5 to 6 pm. On the Bournemouth and Weymouth line there were numerous extras to both destinations plus two or three whole trains to both Lymington and Swanage. On the West of England route each main departure for Exeter and the West was likely to run in anything up to three or four separate parts for various resorts in North and South Devon and Cornwall. All these had to be fitted in between an intensive electric service which also used the fast lines – four trains an hour to Portsmouth Harbour plus two more which ran first stop Surbiton then all stations (on the slow line thereafter) to Woking where they split for Alton and Portsmouth & Southsea. There were, in addition, two further electric services which used the fast lines as far as Surbiton; these were for Guildford via Effingham Junction, first stop Wimbledon then Surbiton. Fitting all these services onto two tracks meant tight headways – two minutes between electrics and three between steam was the rule. Because it was not always easy to identify a particular train on a route the steam services carried a reporting number hung on the

smokebox door in addition to the regular route code discs/lamps. There could thus be three different sets of numerals on the front of the loco – its own number, the reporting number and a duty number pasted onto the discs – provided someone had remembered to do this of course. These pictures give a flavour of what it was like to see the procession of trains in both directions which passed through Surbiton within a couple of hours or so, on 1st August 1964.

Above. Merchant Navy Pacific 35020 BIBBY LINE is working duty No.129 as it arrives at Surbiton in charge of train No.409, the 09.00 Waterloo to Exmouth. Photograph Alistair Nisbet.

Below. Merchant Navy Pacific 35006 PENINSULAR & ORIENT S N Co is heading for Waterloo on duty No.461 with train 219, a Salisbury to Waterloo service. Photograph Alistair Nisbet.

Battle of Britain Pacific 34077 603 SQUADRON on duty 45 powers through the station with the 09.24 Waterloo to Weymouth, train No.410, as holidaymakers await the arrival of their train. Note the regulation blazer and flannels (and tie of course) of the 1960s British male on holiday. Photograph Alistair Nisbet.

West Country Pacific 34092 CITY OF WELLS has charge of the 09.30 Waterloo to Bournemouth West (train No.411) as it calls to pick up a crowd bound for the seaside. There is no duty number on the discs. The train time, helpfully chalked on the smokebox door (as in other illustrations here) added yet further numerals to the front of the locomotive. Photograph Alistair Nisbet.

Empty stock for outbound services could present a problem for Clapham yard and so it was a common sight during the week to see sidings full of coaching sets at places like Esher, Oatlands and Basingstoke which never turned a wheel except on summer Saturdays when they would be pressed into service. Here BR Standard Class 4 2-6-0 76082 takes a rake of empty stock to London – train No.230. Photograph Alistair Nisbet.

Train No.417, the 11.05 Waterloo to Bournemouth West, approaches the station behind BR Class 5 4-6-0 73171, watched by an Inspector standing behind the LIMIT OF SHUNT sign. The duty seems to be No.6. Photograph Alistair Nisbet.

Last N7s of Liverpool Street

By 1960, the year of these two pleasing studies, suburban steam (or steam of any sort really) had little future under the great roofs at Liverpool Street; electrification of the suburban routes out to Enfield, Hertford and so on, came in November and the last of the N7s eked out a wretched existence until 1962. 69699 carrying a 30A Stratford shedplate has arrived with a suburban set while 69725 (it carries a Southend plate) is in charge of the stores train. Photographs A.H. Lucas, The Transport Treasury.

The trains come and go at London Victoria on Saturday, 4 April 1953. Top, they're cleaning the bank of glazing on Victoria (Eastern) signal box – now long closed – as Battle of Britain Pacific 34070 MANSTON rolls into the 'West End' terminus. Below, MANSTON and its train has cleared the view, having run into its platform and another BoB, 34072 257 SQUADRON is revealed, waiting to leave. Both Pacifics are now preserved, on the Swanage Railway. Photographs R.C. Riley, The Transport Treasury.

Pacifics at London Victoria

Above, 257 SQUADRON makes its exit from Victoria and, a while later, MANSTON backs out attached to the rear of its train. Victoria sometimes seemed to share that trance-like quality of Euston and it could seem strangely quite and empty for periods during the day. The empty stock pilot on the far end will be an Ivatt 2-6-2T, an H 0-4-4T or even an E2 0-6-0T – earlier in the year there had been some surprising appearances of an ex-LCDR R class 0-4-4T, 31660. *The Railway Observer* commented that this tank represented a company that had 'ceased to exist for operating purposes 54 years ago'. Photographs R.C. Riley, The Transport Treasury.

Railway Reminiscences:
A Trainspotter's Wanderings in North Lincolnshire in the 1960s
Roger Hockney

Whilst we all know of those exotic trainspotting locations like Edinburgh Waverley or Bristol Temple Meads, there were hundreds of places where the hum-drum life of the railways was pursued anonymously, beyond the reach of our eminent railway photographers. Yet these locations held a wealth of interest as to how the railway supported the local community and ran its day to day business. So what about Grimsby and north Lincolnshire? What passenger and goods trains came and went in this far eastern outpost of both the Great Central and Great Northern Railways? What delights were there for the ardent trainspotter, literally at the end of the line?

The network at Grimsby was based on two main routes; the former GN line to Peterborough opened progressively in 1848 and the former GC one to Sheffield, again progressively, opened in the late 1840s, although Cleethorpes didn't get its first station until 1863. Interestingly, it was the Great Central which made Cleethorpes a resort town, through a £100,000 scheme to rebuild the station, create a promenade, erect swimming baths and even a pier pavilion. Branches sprang from the Great Central route westwards for New Holland and the ferry to Hull and at Barnetby, to Lincoln. The main route to Sheffield itself split into two, via Doncaster or via Retford, at Barnetby. This brief description excludes the complex of local lines around Grimsby and Immingham Docks, both promoted by the local railway companies. The new docks at Immingham, for example, were built by the Great Central and opened by King George V in 1912.

In the 1960s there was a good passenger train service to Doncaster and Sheffield from Grimsby and Cleethorpes, via either Scunthorpe or Gainsborough and Retford. Indeed, in those days, the 'main' line was that from Cleethorpes to Sheffield via Gainsborough, Retford and Worksop. Some services, especially in the summer, were extended to Manchester (London Road), changing locomotives from the ubiquitous Immingham B1 4-6-0 at Sheffield (Victoria) to a Woodhead route electric loco. The Scunthorpe route to Doncaster boasted one of the slowest passenger trains in Britain. In the 1960s, the 5.49am from Doncaster trundled into Cleethorpes at 8.28am.

K1 2-6-0 62063 rests in West Marsh sidings on the outskirts of Grimsby, probably on a freight train from York, on 11 April 1964. By this time, as work contracted, the York-Grimsby freight was one of the longer diagrams for York K1s. 62063 was condemned in September 1964. Photograph Roger Hockney.

the cattle dock at the north end of the station with some sandwiches and a flask. That ruse worked well until on one occasion, the dock was occupied by a wagon loaded with cattle that were increasingly restive in the summer heat. Their discomfiture also distressed mother who announced that this was not a spot she favoured for future visits. The smell and flies must have helped her to come to this view too.

Travelling by train from Grimsby first meant checking what was afoot in the busy sidings at Barnetby. Usually, a Frodingham O4 2-8-0 would be simmering somewhere near the large signalbox at Wraby Junction. Even today, Barnetby and Wraby Junction still draw modern enthusiasts. What with the iron ore trains shuttling back and forth from Immingham Docks to the steelworks at Scunthorpe, coal trains passing through with imported coal for Scunthorpe or the Yorkshire power stations – and the return empties, oil tanks and trains loaded with steel coil etc., passenger trains are in a minority. Gone of course are the O4s, O2s and WDs, replaced originally by Class 20s, 47s, 37s, 31s, 56s and 58s. In their turn these have been replaced by Class 66s in their many variations and Class 60s.

And the mechanical signalling remains. That giant box at Wraby Junction sits half a mile west of the station. Barnetby East box rises at the eastern boundary of the station. Yes, you can close your eyes and imagine. The wires still sing as the signals are pulled off. Is that a WD 2-8-0 drifting down the bank from Melton Ross to the east, iron ore tipplers pushing at the buffers? Sorry, it's a Class 66 on a Doncaster-bound service. The bad news about Barnetby station is that, being constructed as two island platforms, access for disabled passengers has been difficult. The consequence is that a substantial ramped footbridge has been constructed at the eastern end of the station. It's not that it's large but you can see its blue bulk from nearly a mile away, dominating the village, never mind the station. Surely a visually more acceptable solution could have been found that still met the needs of disabled persons?

Scunthorpe is on a ridge so that both eastbound and westbound freights faced a climb, and still do. A Frodingham loco would be based at Gunness Sidings near the River Trent crossing at Althorpe to assist heavy eastbound freight trains into

Scunthorpe. Similarly, assistance could be provided westbound out of the sidings at Barnetby.

The writer's earliest recollections of 'Scunny' are of parking in the car with dad to watch industrial tank engines labour up the slag heaps with wagons of molten material. Vigorous shunting of the loose coupled wagons was necessary to rotate the wagon-mounted cupolas and pour the red hot waste material down the side of the slag heap.

Westbound train journeys past the various works complexes meant trying to observe both sides of the line at the same time. The haul of WDs, O4s, O1s and O2s in a few miles could be substantial. Then, suddenly, one arrived at Scunthorpe station and it was all over. Passenger trains departing the station entered a cutting before descending Gunhouse Bank and running over the Scotter Road Viaduct to Gunness. The River Trent was crossed on the massive King George V lifting Bridge, opened in 1916. Then, it was on to Doncaster, with perhaps some loco interest at the mine sidings around Stainforth and Hatfield.

Trains ran down to Lincoln Central from Grimsby and Cleethorpes, parting company from the Sheffield route at Wraby Junction. Oh, those banks of gantry signals – catch them while you can! The run to Lincoln was a dull one for trainspotters, through agricultural country. There were sixteen stations between Grimsby and Lincoln (Central), a distance of 44 miles, so trains stopped every two to three miles at what were in effect little more than sleepy, gas-lit wayside halts. The main flurry of activity came at Market Rasen, the only station now open between Barnetby and Lincoln, where a smattering of passengers would board or alight. If you were really lucky, there would be a WD in the iron ore sidings at Holton-le-Moor en route, but this was rare.

By the early 1960s, almost all the passenger services on this line were in the hands of Derby 'Heavyweight' DMUs in the 50XXX and 56XXX series running into Lincoln (Central). The summer would be enlivened with the occasional excursion from the Nottingham and Leicester direction to Cleethorpes, although exotic locos from places with strange sounding names rarely appeared on this route. Your writer recalls waiting at Grimsby Town Station with heightened anticipation to see an excursion

The journey of 52 miles was completed in 159 minutes at an average speed of 20 miles per hour.

Retford was very popular with trainspotters. This was because there was a cheap day return on offer that got you from Cleethorpes behind a B1 4-6-0, to the hallowed tracks of the East Coast main line. A day at 'Retty' with some potted meat sandwiches and a bottle of Vimto was the ultimate for north Lincolnshire lads in the summer holidays. Especially favoured was the south end of the station where, at that time, the GN main line and the GC Worksop to Grimsby line crossed on the flat. However, Doncaster was beyond reach for us – no cheap day return ticket from Grimsby was available! That meant persuading dad to get the car out on Sunday and drive there, parking on

Retford K1 2-6-0 62060 ambles away from Retford with a northbound local freight. The Retford K1s supplanted the J11s and J6s on local freights but by the time of the photograph, 30 March 1965, were underemployed. 62060 went to the scrapyard in August 1967, part of the last batch of K1s, all based at Tyne Dock. Photograph Roger Hockney.

from Burton on Trent to Cleethorpes which would have travelled this route. Would it be a Black 5? Or better still a Crab? No, just a Colwick K3!

The single daily Cleethorpes-Birmingham train was, of course, Immingham B1 hauled, but there was an interesting summer Saturdays only service on this route. This was the Leicester (Central) to Cleethorpes train which materialised for a few weeks in high summer, before being cut back to Nottingham (Victoria) for the rest of the summer timetable. It travelled via Mansfield and Edwinstowe to Lincoln on the route of the former Lancashire, Derbyshire and East Coast Railway. Despite the hopes of the local trainspotters at Cleethorpes, this train always failed to live up to expectations. It was invariably a Colwick B1 job.

For a trainspotter from Cleethorpes, Lincoln itself could hold some railway interest. The highlight of the day was to see the two cross-country trains that called there in the late afternoon before the DMU to Cleethorpes and home summoned the hungry trainspotter at 5.17pm. First, the Newcastle-Colchester service arrived at 4.34pm, usually in the hands of a York V2,

followed at 4.51pm by the Liverpool-Harwich. This was the 'Cross Country Continental', once upon a time the preserve of March B17s as far as Sheffield (Victoria). Later, Britannias took over. A B17 was regarded as a rarity by north Lincolnshire lads, so potentially this was a great opportunity to enhance one's collection. Trouble was, March shed would insist on sending the same one, or so it seemed, day after day! 61623 LAMBTON CASTLE seemed to be a particularly popular choice.

Lincoln held other railway interests. The engine shed was adjacent to the Brayford Pool in the centre of the city, so the yard could easily be seen without too much effort. The drawback was that the pedestrian access was over a river so that unofficial access was difficult! The other 'shed' was a little poppet of a building next to St Marks Station. This was the former Midland Railway establishment. Sunday afternoon trips to Lincoln with the parents for a 'sit' at the Brayford Pool and an ice cream could convert into a visit to the peripheries of the main GN shed and a call at the Midland shed at St Mark's, where access was freely available. Usually this meant seeing just one loco, the

Stanier Class 4 tank from Nottingham brewing up to take the 7.18pm to Birmingham, which conveyed mails to Tamworth. Finally, if one were really lucky, Sunday East Coast main line diversions might be in operation bringing East Coast expresses through Lincoln itself.

Trains also ran from Cleethorpes to New Holland (Pier) connecting with the paddle steamers to Hull. A trip on the 'Tattershall Castle', the 'Lincoln Castle' or the 'Wingfield Castle' was something very different. The thump of the engines, the balcony view into the engine room, the ancient lounges with dead flies trapped behind the glass in the pictures on the walls; the few cars shoe-horned onto the deck. Yes, it was an early form of roll-on, roll-off ferry. The standard joke was that the crew were so good at loading cars because they'd trained with sardine packers in Norway.

New Holland had two stations. New Holland (Town) stood on dry land at the beginning of the long jetty out into the River Humber, where stood New Holland Pier. Opened in 1848, Pier Station stood at the end of the 1,000 foot wooden jetty which connected with a floating landing stage, so that ferries could berth at all states of the tide. Services ran from Cleethorpes onto the Pier, calling at Town Station. If the weather was bad, many a foot passenger, having parked the car in the Town station car park, would hop on the train. The walk along the exposed Pier in horizontal rain was not to be lightly contemplated.

Arriving at Hull (Corporation Pier), the trainspotter found he had entered the orange world of the North Eastern Region. Hull Paragon station was still a walk across the city. Parents were more concerned with shopping and trainspotting at Paragon had to wait and wait. I never did get there, so my D49 collection was woefully thin.

Two trains of particular interest ran from Cleethorpes, to Leeds and Birmingham respectively. The 7.00am to Birmingham (New Street) arrived there at 11.13am after travelling via Lincoln St Marks (one of the few trains in the 1960s to use the link to the former Midland Railway station from the GC). It then forged on to Nottingham, Leicester and Hinckley, avoiding Derby. Your writer remembers travelling to Birmingham on this train behind Immingham B1 61379 MAYFLOWER. As the loco penetrated ever deeper into foreign territory, so the cheers of the lineside spotters grew louder. It was

like a royal progress as such a rare 'namer' moved further from home. This train was extended on summer Saturdays, firstly to Bournemouth, but then swapped to Sidmouth and Exmouth, arriving at 5.40pm. The local Lincolnshire lads had never heard of the stations beyond Birmingham and Bristol through which this train would travel, never mind about the rarities that would pull it.

The other service was an interesting 'Mondays, Tuesday, Thursday and Saturdays only' to Leeds (Central). Leaving Cleethorpes at 9.23 am, it avoided Doncaster altogether to call at Thorne (South) then South Elmsall and Wakefield (Westgate) before arriving at Leeds (Central) at 12.05pm. Again, this was an Immingham B1 turn.

Then of course there were the East Lincolnshire line trains to Louth, Boston, Spalding and Peterborough, with two trains a day to Kings Cross. These London trains were notable for the use of Immingham B1s all the way. Some say that this was their most onerous task. The 154 miles were covered in around 3 hours 40 minutes. North of Peterborough, the trains stopped at all principal stations, with 'principal' loosely defined! So Firsby, Willoughby and Alford had a through

service to London as well as Louth, Boston and Spalding. After Peterborough the trains were generally non-stop, taking 100 minutes for a little under 80 miles. The 6.50am from Grimsby was followed by the 8.44am service; they returned at 6.45pm and 4.15pm respectively.

Of course, there were summer and Saturday variations. The summer timetable for 1960 shows a Fridays only mid-day service, for instance, to Kings Cross. In the summer, the local lads were also treated to the Saturdays only trains from Leeds and Bradford to Skegness which could be non-stop through Grimsby Town station, then down the East Lincs. line to Firsby, before taking the branch to Skegness. These services brought Leeds and Bradford locos to the Grimsby-Peterborough line, usually B1s, though Black 5s could also make an appearance.

What if the trainspotter wanted to stay 'at home'? What delights were there to be savoured courtesy of the faithful Dawes bicycle? Cleethorpes station slept in the winter, its six long platforms underused whilst the nearby carriage sidings at New Clee and Suggitts Lane were permanently full of resting carriages. Doubtless these were the very carriages used

WD 90029 draws to a halt in West Marsh Sidings, Grimsby with a Class E freight, in which fish empties appear to predominate, 14 September 1964. The competition lurks in the background while the ubiquitous yellow high visibility jacket has not yet arrived on the scene. Photograph Roger Hockney.

for those briefly flowering summer Saturdays only services. In the winters of the early 1960s, the resident Lincoln-based Derby Heavyweight DMUs ran the show, bar a few steam operated services. The Kings Cross, Birmingham and Leeds trains were all B1 hauled, the Kings Cross services soon to be taken over by a stud of Britannias from Norwich. The winter 5.58pm to Doncaster was hauled by a 'Donny' B1, doubtless the return working of the 5.49am stopper from Doncaster. This steam service seemed to endure and endure, when all passenger services around were being dieselised.

There was a 'rush hour' for steam in the winter, though. Promising to be back for tea, one cycled down to the station at around 5pm to see two workmen's trains (well, actually one was workwomen's). One originated at Immingham Dock and the other from Great Coates, the first station out of Grimsby westwards and the base for a biscuit factory. I know little more, so further details of these trains would be appreciated. So around 5.30pm of a winter's evening no less than three B1s would be in the station. The two works trains with their suburban non-corridor carriages arrived close behind each other around 5.30pm, plus the Doncaster service usually

in platform 5 awaiting its 5.58pm departure. Three steam locos might not seem a lot, but there were lengthy periods in those winter days in the early 1960s when there would be no steam locos in evidence at all.

All this changed for the better from Easter onwards as the weekend excursions started to appear. At the height of the season in the early 1960s, *forty* expresses could arrive within the space of a few hours, all needing servicing and their engines turning on the Cleethorpes vacuum-operated turntable. The variety of locomotives widened dramatically. The usual suspects were joined by Crabs, Black 5s, Standard 5s and, on one auspicious day, three Jubilees. V2s were also known to make spasmodic appearances towards The End.

Then there was Grimsby and its fish trains. In the early 1960s, before cod wars and the advent of road haulage, Grimsby was the place (sorry!) to be to see fish trains. They have been much documented. Like many aspects of rail operations, this was sophisticated in the extreme, with precision loading of trains with boxes of iced fish for despatch all over the country. Trains left precisely to time, hurrying past in a heady mix of steamy and fishy smells. Conversely, empty wagons found their way back as part of a

never ending, or so we thought then, circuit of use. Looked at from the point of view of the trainspotter, there would be no great surprises in the engines provided. Immingham locos tended to predominate, with the exception of the 4.48pm fish to Nottingham, which was a 16A duty, usually bringing a Midland 4F to the seaside. In later years Crabs, Black 5s or the occasional Standard 4-6-0 could turn up.

So, after school, it was off on the bike to Grimsby Docks Station to watch. First there was the tender-first cavalcade from Immingham shed of locos coupled together, entering the Docks complex, to attach to their trains. The procession across the Cleethorpe Road level crossing out of the Docks and through the Dock Station started at 4.30pm with the Whitland fish. (Talk about coals to Newcastle... though I wonder just how many of those fish wagons actually found their way to Whitland). This would be B1 or K3 hauled (later Britannias took over). Immingham always managed to keep a few of its K3s clean and one usually turned up on this job.

The Nottingham fish followed hard on its heels, then at 5.13pm it was the turn of the Manchester fish to Aston Moss. Again this was a K3 job that became one for a Britannia or

WD 90223 under repair in the former GN shed at Retford on 30 March 1965. The locomotive was withdrawn within months. Perhaps this was in effect the end of the line and it never returned to service. Photograph Roger Hockney.

WD 90133 makes for Barnetby from Scunthorpe with coke empties on 21 September 1965. The fact that it is running tender first with brake vans topping and tailing the train suggests reversal at Barnetby before heading west towards Worksop and Sheffield. The 2-8-0 has just months left, for it was withdrawn before the end of the year. Photograph Roger Hockney.

an Immingham 9F in due course. The 5.30pm to London headed off down the GN line to Peterborough behind K3s then the Immingham Britannias or 9Fs. There was a lull then until the Leicester at 6.25pm, a London service at 7.00pm and an 8.25pm to Leeds. Of course schoolboys were expected to bike home for tea, so the 5.30pm departure effectively brought down the curtain on the proceedings.

Grimsby Town Station also had something to offer. The bike ride from home meant this was a school holiday destination during the week or a Saturday trip. Trapped between two level crossings, the three platform station was tightly constrained. Effectively two platforms were used for through trains (the main platform and the outer face of the island platform) while the inner face of the island platform was used for arrivals and departures down the East Lincolnshire line, almost all of which terminated at Town Station. Two goods avoiding lines skirted past the outer face of the island platform.

Any train calling at the station with more than seven carriages would foul a level crossing. This usually meant the London trains. Some originated at Cleethorpes and then were faced with reversal at Town Station. Many a B1 has straddled one of the level crossings for what the (then comparatively few) motorists must have felt was an eternity, while another B1 was hooked on the London-bound end of the train. These activities usually took place early in the day, before breakfast and were missed by most trainspotters, although the Fridays only summer service could be viewed causing its usual disruption at midday.

By the early 1960s, a day at Grimsby Town would see a procession of Lincoln-based Derby Heavyweight DMUs plus a few Cravens units interspersed, especially in the summer, with excursions and 'dated' trains, hauled by B1s, Class 5s and strangers like Crabs or Standard 4-6-0s, plus of course the fish trains. But Grimsby did offer the possibility of other types of freight, attractions which were virtually non-existent at Cleethorpes. This meant loaded iron ore tipplers from the ironstone mines of the East Midlands clanking through off the East Lincolnshire line behind Scunthorpe and Immingham O4s, O1s and WDs, or Doncaster O2s. Empties returned the same way.

There was also a healthy traffic to and from Scunthorpe conveying track ballast to the south. Added to this were a variety of steel trains and empties, general merchandise and, in the season, sugar beet trains heading to the factory at Brigg. Again, 2-8-0s predominated, though Immingham Britannias could appear on general merchandise trains and your writer remembers seeing a J6 struggling valiantly through Grimsby Town with a heavy beet train, steam leaking from every joint. The predictable procession of 2-8-0s on freights was punctuated by the arrival of the daily goods from York which would bring a 50A B16 into Grimsby. In time K1 2-6-0s took over as the B16s disappeared to the scrapheap.

So what would you see now? Well, the large signalbox and mechanical signalling at Cleethorpes have gone, together with the turntable, to be replaced by colour light signalling controlled from Pasture Street Box in Grimsby. The station has been reduced from six platforms to three, its buildings are in need of a coat of paint and sand drifts over the disused rails serving what were platforms 5 and 6. Yet Cleethorpes, Grimsby Town and Scunthorpe still have a healthy (mostly hourly)

B1 4-6-0 61082 lifts the 2.52pm to Boston out of Grimsby Town station across Garden Street level crossing on 1 November 1960. The signals are off for the East Lincs. route, curving to the right behind the signal box. The signalmen has been late in locking the wicket gates! 61082 had been a long-term Immingham resident since May 1947, when it was eight months old. It was scrapped at the end of 1962. Photograph Roger Hockney.

B1 61158 accelerates across the Cleethorpe Road Junction level crossing past the Dock Offices and on to Cleethorpes with a train from Doncaster on 4 September 1963. The train has just left Grimsby Docks Station. 61158 had been a Doncaster engine since 1953 and was condemned there in April 1966. Photograph Roger Hockney.

service of trains to Manchester via Doncaster. Passenger trains start from Grimsby Town for the run to Lincoln Central and beyond to Birmingham, and sometimes further afield. The great survivor must be the New Holland branch and its Barton on Humber appendage, still enjoying an interval service from Cleethorpes. The construction of the Humber Bridge has not seen it off, although the Pier at New Holland is closed. Grimsby Docks Station is an unstaffed halt on the single line now remaining from Grimsby Town to Cleethorpes. Freight trains may be prolific at Barnetby and Immingham, but little reaches Grimsby itself. The direct route to Sheffield via Gainsborough slumbers gently so far as passengers and freight are concerned. The

passenger service from Retford via Gainsborough Central to Grimsby only operates on Saturdays with three return trains, though there are Lincoln to Doncaster trains serving Gainsborough Lea Road. At least it has fared better than the East Lincs. route south out of Grimsby, now occupied by a new road on Grimsby's outskirts. For those interested in mechanical signalling, semaphores still predominate in the wider area, with the exception of part of the Grimsby/Cleethorpes district.

Certainly all is not lost. Visitors will still find much of interest and, remember, steam still lives on in Lincolnshire at the Lincolnshire Wolds Railway, based at Ludborough Station, between Louth and Grimsby. In Cleethorpes itself, the Cleethorpes Coast Light Railway

goes from strength to strength, attracting visitors to admire the locos from the former Sutton Park Miniature Railway. The Appleby-Frodingham Railway Society runs steam hauled tours around the Scunthorpe Steelworks complex. If these are not your style, then go to Barnetby, listen to the singing of the signal wires... and imagine!

Grimsby's minaret-like dock tower is on the horizon as B1 4-6-0 61168 passes the remains of New Clee sidings with the 2.28pm Fridays only workmen's train from Great Coates and Immingham on 18 September 1964. Cleethorpes station is five minutes away. 61168 arrived at Immingham in 1953 and was condemned there in October 1965. Photograph Roger Hockney.

B1 4-6-0 61031 REEDBUCK lifts the summer Saturdays only Bradford/Leeds-Skegness southwards out of Grimsby along the East Lincs. line on 29 August 1964. A Copley Hill engine for a few months at the time of the photograph, it was to be transferred to Ardsley within a few weeks and be condemned by November 1964. Photograph Roger Hockney.

Lincoln Central station has thankfully survived major 'modernisation'. On 4 September 1964 long-time Doncaster resident B1 61157 having arrived with empty coaching stock, ambles through the station towards the infamous High Street crossing. The two car DMU has arrived from Retford. Photograph Roger Hockney.

On 26 August 1961 there was a shortage of motive power in West Yorkshire and LMR 8F 2-8-0 48615 has been pressed into duty on a Wakefield Kirkgate-Cleethorpes excursion. It is about to enter Grimsby Town station. Photograph Roger Hockney.

K3 2-6-0 61912 with cattle empties on 11 February 1961, about to cross Littlefield Lane level crossing and enter Grimsby Town station. An Immingham engine, it moved on to Lincoln, then Kings Cross to become, in 1962, a stationary boiler. Eventual withdrawal came in 1965, three years after the last of the K3s had been taken out of running stock. Photograph Roger Hockney.

Doncaster wasn't just A4s and prestigious expresses! L1 2-6-4T 67787 does the bread and butter work of station pilot on 9 August 1961. It has detached a fish van from a DMU, doubtless from Hull or Grimsby. Photograph Roger Hockney.

Immingham took pride in the seven Britannia Pacifics. Here a very clean 70037 HEREWARD THE WAKE enters Grimsby Docks station at the head of the 4.30pm fish train to Whitland on 13 March 1962. Photograph Roger Hockney.

An O1 2-8-0, 63725, picks its way towards Whisker Hill Junction, Retford, at the head of an eastbound coal train on 23 September 1964. The earthworks for the dive under the East Coast Main Line are well advanced. Photograph Roger Hockney.

While B1 4-6-0 61385 awaits departure from Cleethorpes with the 1.46pm Saturday only to Leeds and Bradford, the crew pass the time trackside, on 15 August 1964. Photograph Roger Hockney.

K3 2-6-0 61889 races out of Grimsby, towards Pasture Street level crossing with the 4.30pm Whitland fish on 13 July 1962. This was its swansong; it was condemned by November 1962. Photograph Roger Hockney.

York B16/3 61463 enters Grimsby with the daily freight from York. It is 12 April 1962 and this service will soon transfer to K1 haulage. Photograph Roger Hockney.

O2/2 2-8-0 63937 brings iron ore tipplers through Grimsby Town station on 13 April 1961. It has come off the East Lincs. line and will head via Barnetby to Scunthorpe. A Grimsby-Cleethorpes Transport AEC Regent III leans to the bend above the O2. The long-term station pilot, D3709, rests in the cattle dock. Photograph Roger Hockney.

While Britannias became commonplace in the north-west on lowly freights towards the end of steam, this is 4 March 1961 and 70040 CLIVE OF INDIA has just arrived at Immingham along with several others displaced by EE Type 4s from East Anglian services. It is passing through Grimsby Town Station with a freight off the East Lincs. line, probably bound for West Marsh Sidings. Photograph Roger Hockney.

Resident Immingham B1 61168 ambles away from Barnetby towards Melton Ross with eastbound empties on 27 August 1965, probably heading for Immingham. The four track section between Barnetby and Brocklesby was reduced to two and subsequently the westbound slow line from Immingham has been reinstated. Photograph Roger Hockney.

B1 4-6-0 61055 hurries west out of Retford and approaches Whisker Hill Junction in the distance, with a mixed freight on 23 September 1964. Photograph Roger Hockney.

On 23 September 1964, late in the afternoon, 61157 heads north past Retford North Junction – from the look of the second interesting coach, it could be empty stock for Doncaster. The B1 was scrapped from there in September 1965. Photograph Roger Hockney.

With the crew on lookout, O4/1 63692 in the typical O4 livery of mottled grime, drifts towards Whisker Hill Junction, Retford on 23 September 1964. The signalled route will take it across the infamous flat crossing and doubtless onto the former GC Shed at Thrumpton. Photograph Roger Hockney.

Steam On Shed:
Late Days at Gloucester Horton Road
By Peter Kerslake

On 4 January 1965 Class 9F 2-10-0 No.92138 rests at Horton Road shed; the bunker of a 41XX 2-6-2T is visible on the right. The view is towards the east ('Horton Road' itself ran north-south past the rear of the shed) and this is the six road section, added some years after the original shed. This stood to the right, and was a shorter but loftier four road affair. Photograph Peter Kerslake.

Though looking very much the worse for wear on 4 January 1965 Hall 4-6-0 No.5936 OAKLEY HALL retains number and nameplates in this, the final year of Western Region steam. This engine had been at Old Oak Common in an earlier life but the 85B plate reveals her to be now on the Horton Road complement. Photograph Peter Kerslake.

One of the foremost examples of the original batch of Great Western Halls, No.4920 DUMBLETON HALL by the Horton Road turntable, on 4 January 1965. No.4920 still has numberplates but her nameplates have gone, in common with many of her surviving sister engines at this period. At one time a Taunton engine, No.4920 was saved from the cutters' torches at Barry in South Wales and rescued for preservation. Don Breckon, the celebrated painter of West Country railway scenes, featured this engine in his painting of her leaving Kingswear and proceeds of sale of prints went towards the restoration fund. Photograph Peter Kerslake.

The view from Horton Road, where there was a level crossing, in January 1965. The taller and original four road shed rises beyond (its roof in a terrible state) and we can peer across to the yard where stands the GW-style coal stage, added only relatively late, in the early 1920s. The struggling Hall is 7915 MERE HALL, without nameplates. Photograph Peter Kerslake.

London Midland Class 5 No.44776 on shed at Horton Road, on 19 January 1965. The old Midland Railway roundhouse, a short distance away at Barnwood, had passed to the WR in 1958 but had closed in 1964 – thereafter it was used for storing withdrawn engines only. No.44776 was at Saltley in earlier days and may well be still stationed there at this date. Photograph Peter Kerslake.

Rugby 8F 2-8-0 No.48437 basking in the late afternoon sun at Horton Road, 19 January 1965. Photograph Peter Kerslake.

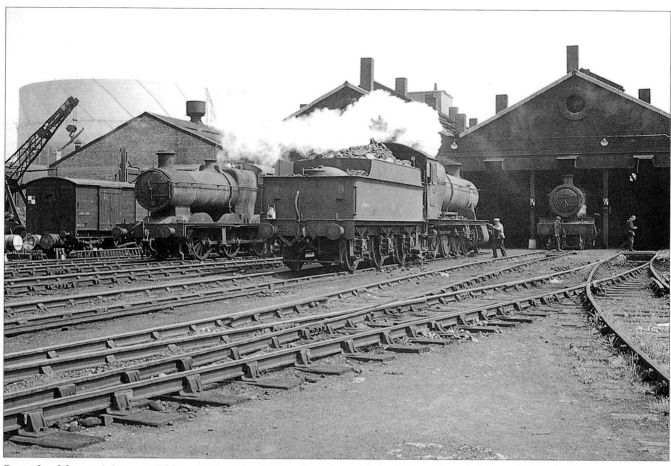

Some healthy activity on 20 May 1965, with plenty of smoke and clanking noises belying the shed's imminent decline (it closed to steam with effect from the first day of 1966). The 0-6-0, No.2242, forms a pleasant portrait outside the shed while 2-8-0 3820 makes more of a show of it, blowing off with a full head of steam as it readies to leave the yard. 6829 BURMINGTON GRANGE peers out from the shed. Photograph Peter Kerslake.

On the turntable on 4 September 1964 is 7815 FRITWELL MANOR; a former Worcester engine, it now appears to carry an 87, Neath District, plate. Even at this time the engine still has her nameplates and number plates and appears to be in a reasonable condition. Photograph Peter Kerslake.

Not so fortunate as 7815, however, was one of the original series of Castles, sad 4093 DUNSTER CASTLE. On this very day she has lost all plates and this was her last day in steam. Readers of *British Railways Illustrated* may recall that in a February 2003 issue we saw her numberplates being removed and in this shot, stripped of all identity and a shadow of her former self, she is now ready to move off Horton Road in steam, 'light engine' for the sidings at Hempstead to await a move to a breaking yard. A former Landore engine, she would have worked from South Wales to Paddington on many of the express passenger services in happier times, in pristine condition, no doubt. Photograph Peter Kerslake.

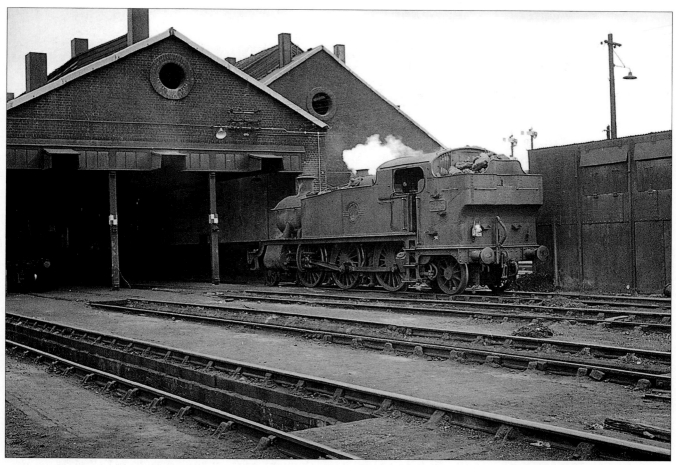

Early afternoon on 2 July 1965, mid-way through the final year of steam on the Western and 6113, an Oxford engine of former days, sits outside Horton Road shed. Photograph Peter Kerslake.

Pannier tank 3643, once of Bristol St. Phillip's Marsh, makes a pleasing study on 2 July 1965. Photograph Peter Kerslake.

ROADE STATION - A 1950s View
(with a bit of history thrown in) By Graham Onley

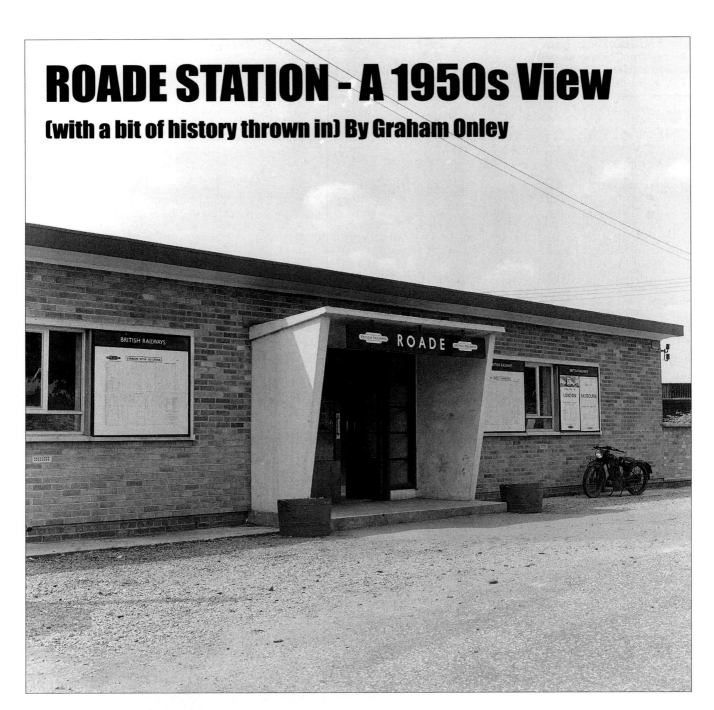

As a spotter through most of the 1950s, Roade station was the place to be if I could manage to escape the confines of Duston West Junction, Northampton. Well, on second thoughts, given any choice, I might just have settled for 12 months at Carlisle Citadel! The whole point of this is that in truth, young as I was, the only thing that really interested me was getting as many new numbers in as short a time as possible. The surroundings of Roade station, like those of every other station I had ever set foot in, on or near, went completely unnoticed until the 1960s had kicked off.

It would, for instance, have been about 1960 before I noticed that the entrance hall to Roade station was obviously more modern in design than the rest of the premises... That said, I admit to having about the same lack of knowledge long after the place had been obliterated by British Railways at the time of the west coast electrification. I have to admit further to having never set foot in the station booking hall, for I never had cause to travel to Roade by train. I do admit to spending plenty of time on the platforms, almost certainly only after the premises had reached their final condition.

In recent years I have, like many a spotter maturing into a photographer, turned my attention to what is left of the old railway wherever I might find myself, not just in my home area. Naturally, this has led me to attempt to discover just what I had previously "seen",

but ignored in my (unconsummated) quest for 46102 BLACK WATCH. (Would it ever be next in the interminable procession of rebuilt Scots racing up or down the main line?) So when a set of photographs of Roade station turned up, taken on at least two different occasions, I was fascinated.

As you've probably gathered, I had not realised that Roade station had ever looked any different to the one I had all but ignored during the 1950s. However, I soon appreciated that a measure of renewal of some worn out or merely unfashionable parts of the station had taken place during that blessed decade. Some readers may recollect a series of photographs taken in Roade Cutting and to the south of Roade station around August 1953, which appeared in "BRILL" Annual No.10, celebrating Christmas 2001. I would hazard a guess that the photographs of the modernised/refurbished/renewed Roade station were taken on the same date. Unsurprisingly, it is likely that those of the station in disarray during its cosmetic attention were taken sometime previously!

It would seem that the work involved renewal of the timbers of the footbridge, the gutting of the waiting rooms, and the removal of the surviving canopies over the platforms, which can only be seen with certainty to have been over the up slow and part of the down fast line platforms. Prior to this particular period of renewal, all platforms may have had some level of cover, but the photographs are not conclusive. Repointing of the brickwork of the platform above rail level has clearly been a timely part of the task. It does seem a pity that the new entrance hall, a cross between Festival of Britain and Coronation styles, managed to engineer the loss of the ROADE STATION name picked out in the brickwork below and to the north of the old entrance hall, and which was in turn above what appears to have been the booking office.

An additional strip of modern concrete slabs had also been inserted inside the platform edge coping stones, reducing the acreage of original black herringbone style paving common to many a 'nor-western' station platform.

Roade station had a fairly long life, but was probably not in the higher echelons when the incoming pennies were counted. It was this that was no doubt instrumental in its demise with effect from 7 September 1964 for passenger traffic, and 6 July of the same year for goods. It could be said that the long life was mainly due to its early opening, 17 September 1838 for First and Second class passengers and parcels, with goods traffic following from 12 November 1838. Third class passengers had to wait until 5 October 1840! Either way, there was approximately 126 years of passenger service. The slow line platforms would have followed with the opening of the Northampton loop (still known to railwaymen as the "new line").

The first trains to pass *through* Roade were from 24 June 1838, after the opening of Kilsby Tunnel on 21 June 1838. Before this time, passengers to and from the north were conveyed on road coaches along what is now the A5 Watling Street. Roade station also became a jumping off point for Northampton, using road coaches, and this continued until the opening of Northampton Bridge Street station on the Blisworth to Peterborough line in 1845. Once Blisworth station was in use, Roade would have become much less important for Northampton passengers.

I would like to add my thanks to my long time friend in all things, Barry Taylor, for his valued assistance in putting together some of the more factual parts of this effort. The photographs, some of which show before and after scenes, are as follows:

Left 1A and below 1B. **The new entrance to the booking hall and platforms. The posters above the, even then, veteran motor cycle, refer to "Cheap trips to London" on August Bank Holiday Monday and to Eastbourne on the Sunday, which can be seen with the help of a glass to be 7 August, making the year 1955. This could either mean that the Roade cutting and south of Roade station views of 1953 referred to earlier were not taken at the same time as those of the station refurbishment, or that the official photographer did not pay Roade a visit during 1954. Yet the typical jobbing builder's messy application of the pointing cement for the new paving slabs as seen in picture 2A looks a little clean to have been possibly two years old...**

2A. Looking north along the down main line platform 1 from the north end after rebuilding. Paintwork looking spruce, but not particularly glossy, possibly supporting my contention in caption 1. We have not been able to find reference to the dates that refurbishment was carried out. Perhaps an older reader will write... The start of the famous cutting can be seen beyond the second overbridge. More support for the 1953/1955 theory – note the smoke-blackened new paint on the main line side of the footbridge.

2B. Looking north again, from a little further south with dismantling of the old fabric well under way, although no repointing of the platform wall had been attempted. Note the awning surrounding the "Gentlemen" on the down main line platform. Also that 2C reveals the building itself to have been demolished, leaving only what would seem to be a waiting room reduced to a size more in keeping with the expected clientele, and which is a matching pair with the one exactly opposite on the up slow line platform. Sensibly, the waiting room on the centre platform serving two lines is somewhat larger, and even more sensibly a new brick built "Gents" will be seen in picture 2C. Someone has ensured a decent show of flowers in the resurrected flower beds, but there appears to be no gas or electric lighting in the skeletal original lamp standards!

2C. Almost the same viewpoint as 2B, but after completion of the job, as described in 2B. Note the "George Hotel" which introduced many a spotter to his first shandy, and in which even as recently as 2003 I found it difficult to sit in a group reminiscing about the past for fear of missing "something on the main", a thought best kept to oneself! On the other hand, who said history starts today? A closer view of the Waiting Room on the right, over on Platform 1, follows in 2D.

2D, and the Waiting Room on Platform 1.

3A and 3B. Before and After... This is the view from underneath the overbridge carrying the A508 Stony Stratford to Market Harborough via Northampton road. Much of what can be seen here was to disappear, including the surviving LMS station signs and notice boards, examples of which can be seen at the bottom of the footbridge and on the side of the waiting room respectively. The facilities underneath the ancient ROADE STATION letters were to be bricked in completely.

4A and 4B show before and after views of the footbridge over the slow lines and the new booking hall under construction. The lower part of the footbridge on the far side, the up slow platform, was clearly covered and it would not be unreasonable to accept that this applied throughout. I doubt that the advertisements exhorting us to buy CWS goods, and to eat Pascall's sweets survived, nor I suppose the wooden ROADE sign, which was one of dozens replaced by shiny new London Midland region maroon standard types. Another ten years and I suspect that even they disappeared, possibly before anyone thought too hard about collecting for the future. It seems that much of the old footbridge has been re-used.

5. The completed refurbished station viewed, first, from the top of the down main line section of the substantial, but open air new footbridge and then down on Platform 1 and Platform 4. All is quiet for a few moments, save for the porter going about his business along the up main platform. The reason for the insertion of a row of paving slabs into the platform surface? Clever? Or bizarre, given how low the Roade porter's convenience ranked in the scheme of things. Note also Roade Junction signal box, which came into being with the quadrupling of the line from Bletchley and the opening of the Roade-Northampton Castle-Rugby "new" line in 1881, peeping over the (pedestrian only) footbridge at the south end of the station. It was through the round top arch to the right of the main lines that the connection from the SMJR ran into the station, but which never actually opened for passengers (as described in BRILL Annual number 10).

PLATFORM
1

6A and 6B. Standing on the up slow platform, looking north towards the cutting and an eventual arrival at Northampton Castle. Note that the slow line platforms were not considered worthy of the extra row of paving slabs as were the main line platforms. The main line platforms shared with those of the slow line, according to the 1954 summer timetable, six up and nine down services on weekdays, seven up and eight down on Saturdays, with two up and two down on Sundays. The trains involved were a mix of Bletchley to Rugby main line trains, or those emanating from Northampton, which may have travelled either direct (the "new" line) or via Blisworth, which would therefore have involved a stop at the main line platform. The summer of 1939 showed sixteen down and thirteen up trains, most of which travelled via Northampton. This number included a Northampton to Roade push and pull shuttle, running only at peak times, and usually managed by a suitably equipped ex-LNWR 2-4-2 tank.

7. Last look from the station, a pleasing overall view showing something of the semi-rural locale and 'Bridge 205' at the south end.

8. *Note by Patrick Spen:* 'Bridge 205' and the works at the south end – such a contrast to the fields on the west side in 1959. Only one siding is listed at Roade for this period, for the 'Pianoforte Supplies Co.' which seems unlikely. The scene is typical of the pre-electrification, steam railway we still had then, with a sprouting multitude of posts, bins, huts, tanks, gates and all the rest. There are no less than six huts/cabinets in this view alone. Crossing the LNW main line on that slender bridge in the distance is the Stratford on Avon & Midland Joint which connected Ravenstone Wood Junction (Bedford to Northampton) and Towcester. Stored on it and barely visible, just to the left of the bridge, are a line of wagons.

9. *Note by Patrick Spen:* 'Bridge 205' was there to afford access to the works and here it is in all its glorious detail, a straightforward girder overbridge with a simple circular brick arch within the abutment structure. It probably began life as an accommodation bridge.

10. *Note by Patrick Spen:* Looking north towards the station in 1959. The track on the left looks to be a down refuge, with its exit controlled only by a diminutive LNW-type ground signal to its right.

11. *Note by Patrick Spen:* In the days when a strip of blasted heath (if anything upright survives it is covered in graffiti) runs alongside most of our main lines, we cannot fail to appreciate these 1950s views, with every corner crammed with stock and the detritus and paraphernalia of constant commerce and activity. Clearly those two wagons are off the daily pick-up goods, serving the works at its own loading dock. Heaven!

THIRTIES FILE

'AULD REEKIE'
By Bryan Wilson

This is North British signalling artistry at the west end of Waverley station. As was the company's custom, the spectacle plates were painted white. Modellers should, however, carefully note the detail differences. The weight bars are of different types as are the finials; one is the Stevens 'open ball' and the other a 'cruciform'. The pulley wheels with wires to left and right are unusual and the gantry is attached to the telegraph pole. Below is a North British ground disc on which, when operated, the front flap dropped allowing a white light to be shown (green by LNER days). Two more, of the same variety, protect the adjacent siding outlet. The elegant speed restriction board applying to the Down Main is located so as to apply to both platform ends. Photograph W.D.M. Stephen, The Transport Treasury.

Following the completion of the Forth Bridge in 1890, all traffic from Edinburgh for the north via Fife, having previously used the Granton - Burntisland ferry, suddenly found itself concentrated at the opposite end of Waverley station. Yet, from Corstorphine Junction (to the west of Haymarket) there was only one up and one down line available for the increased traffic. The problem of congestion came to a head during the Edinburgh Trades Holiday in July of that year when trains could be seen standing at every signal from Corstorphine Junction inward. (Corstorphine Junction was re-named Saughton Junction about 1902).

The North British Railway directors decided that 'something must be done'. What was required was a radical reconstruction of Waverley station, together with four tracking from Saughton Junction in the west to Portobello Junction in the east. The station was rebuilt between 1892 and 1900 and the quadrupling completed between Haymarket East and Waverley on 7 July 1895.

The City fathers were not, as can be imagined, keen to see more of Princes Street gardens lost and it was only by invoking the powers of Parliament that the North British was able to proceed with the new works. Nevertheless, screens of

trees were planted to placate the objectors. The two new tracks were laid to the south of the original one. The new works also involved the reconstruction of Haymarket station, including two additional platforms.

At the Mound tunnel at the west end of Waverley, there were more difficulties. The Mound is really an artificial embankment across the old Nor' Loch. The National Gallery of Scotland stands above the railway here and the new line had to pass through the embankment without disturbing the buildings. This was achieved by making a single line tunnel on each side of the existing double bore. The whole works were

This is how the additional (1895) lines penetrated the Mound embankment beneath the National Gallery – a single line tunnel each side of the original one. We are looking westward from Waverley station. What a display of point rodding and cranks, with the signal wires like strands of knitting wool along the wall. Photograph W.D.M. Stephen, The Transport Treasury.

Above. A close-up of the locking mechanisms and fouling bars at the west end of Waverley station. The bar is designed to operate for both directions. Any loco or vehicles depressing it would prevent the signalman from moving the points under them. And who's been cleaning their fire in the station area? Photograph W.D.M. Stephen, The Transport Treasury.

completed on 7 July 1895 with the necessary new signalling controlled by new boxes at Princes Street Gardens and Waverley West (Haymarket East had been renewed on 28 April that year). Trains for both Glasgow and Fife routes could now depart and run in parallel to Saughton Junction.

We are extremely fortunate that W.D.M. Stephen, a Signalling Engineer, photographed the section concerned, with great attention to detail, before the power scheme came in.

Left. More detail for modellers, this time it's signal wire detection in close-up. The wire to the signal passes through the detector slides which ensure that the signal cannot be cleared unless the points are in the correct position. The clearance bar in the foreground was usually of tee shaped section, operated by the lifting clips placed along the length of the bar. When the lever is pulled, the clip rises in an arc, lifting the bar to the level of the rail, then falls to the end of the arc. If a vehicle was standing on the bar, the clip was prevented from rising and the plunger could not be withdrawn, thus the points could not be altered. Note the slots in the tie bar that locate the 'normal' or 'reverse' position. The numbers attached to the sleeper (it looks like 182) refer to the lever in the box. These were attached to the sleepers on the side for which the points laid 'normal' i.e., with the lever in the frame. Photograph W.D.M. Stephen, The Transport Treasury.

A close-up of the trap points in the Up South line between Princes Street Gardens Box and the Mound tunnel. These protected any running back movements when the Down South to Down North junction was being used. The treadle bar can be clearly seen preventing the points from being moved if occupied. Photograph W.D.M. Stephen, The Transport Treasury.

Another superb gantry, looking west from Waverley. The lines from left to right in the tunnels are 'Down South, Up South, Down North and Up North'. The tall arms read along the Down South and Down North, the separate Distants apply to crossing movements from South to North and vice versa at Princes Street Gardens box and the lone home signal applies from the Up South in the wrong direction to the Down North. The lower 'hammer headed' arms are 'shunt ahead' signals and the smaller arms on the ground control local shunting movements. The Up line signals are strung above the tunnel mouth to enable reasonable sighting from the far end. Photograph W.D.M. Stephen, The Transport Treasury.

More signal detail, this time an insight into 'slotting' – in simple terms, not letting the distant clear until the home signal has cleared. The balance weight nearest the post is connected to the home or starting signal and to the lever frame in the box; the centre arm is connected to the Distant signal arm only. The outer balance weight arm connects only to the lever of the box in advance, but not to a signal arm. Clearance of the Home signal leaves the centre arm clear to move by gravity when the Distant lever is pulled at the box in advance. When the Home signal is replaced to danger, the cross piece on the centre arm is also raised, thus restoring the distant to caution. Indeed, a feature of signalling not often seen in close-up. Photograph W.D.M. Stephen, The Transport Treasury.

Princes Street Gardens Box, designed to be in keeping with its environment. The plate beneath the nameboard reads 'Railway Signal Co, Liverpool'. The box contained 45 levers and was the second one with this name. It came into use with the quadrupling on 7 July 1895 and closed on 11 Oct 1936, after which its functions were taken over by the new power installation at Waverley West. Photograph W.D.M. Stephen, The Transport Treasury.

An end view of Princes Street Gardens Box with St Cuthberts Church and the Caledonian Hotel beyond. The signal wire detector slides are mounted on the sleeper ends. Their method of operation in relation to the movement of the facing points can be clearly seen. Photograph W.D.M. Stephen, The Transport Treasury.

We are now facing Haymarket tunnel with the Caledonian Hotel and St Cuthberts rising up towards us. A fine gantry with just the two Down distant arms but banner repeaters telling the state of Haymarket's Down homes due to the intervention of the tunnel. In the Up direction the arms cater for both straight running and movement both ways through Princes Street Gardens junctions. Again the signal post finials are a mixture of open balls and cruciforms. Photograph W.D.M. Stephen, The Transport Treasury.

And finally, back to Waverley and to the Down Main platform (now 10/11). A D34 4-4-0, which through the best glass available looks like 9504 GLEN ALADALE, a long-standing St Margarets engine, has brought empty stock in from Craigentinny. Another fine North British gantry protects the middle crossover lines, note the difference in spectacle dimensions between 'main' and 'subsidiary' arms. The array of advertisements includes some old friends but, inevitably north of the border, Scotts Porage Oats are represented. Does anyone remember 'Oxade', or is that another Scottish delicacy? Photograph W.D.M. Stephen, The Transport Treasury.

DANCE at the ORCHID

The Southern had a small but varied collection of heavy tank engines, of a type and/or look barely known elsewhere. They weren't all that easy to track down either. For a start a lot of their activity took place in that remote and threatening archipelago otherwise known as south and west London. They would seem to have been perfect for ECS at the various SR London termini and though the W 2-6-4Ts, for instance, were actually permitted in all of them (the exception being certain tracks at Charing Cross) they appeared on such work hardly at all. Being occupied with freight, a fair amount of what they did took place at night and when employed in daylight they would, likely as not, be engaged on obscure lines or lurking in unheard-of suburban goods yards. Take W 2-6-4T 31921 at what we assume to be Purley (*DANCE at the ORCHID BALLROOM PURLEY* says the sign) for instance, in 1958. This was typical habitat for these exotic creatures. Below, H16 4-6-2T 30518 is in a more public environment. This, we take it, is Clapham Junction, where one of these striking beasts had a shunting duty for many years, as well as ECS work into Waterloo. Photographs A.H. Lucas, The Transport Treasury. Thanks to Ted Crawforth.

Bishops Stortford and Beyond

By Bryan Wilson

Bishops Stortford has always been a 'frontier point'. It was the terminus of the Northern & Eastern Railway in 1842 until it was extended northwards three years later, in 1845; it was the London Transport boundary with their country buses and Green Line coaches venturing no further and it was the terminus of the Cambridge line outer suburban services from Liverpool Street.

With North East London modernisation in November 1960, it again became the limit of electrification, this time for 26½ years until its continuation to Cambridge. Bishops Stortford was the boundary between the Stratford and Cambridge Districts with South Box reporting to both Control offices but North only dealing with Cambridge. This boundary subsequently moved to Elsenham to give London more control over services approaching the electrified area.

The 'facilities' were never really appropriate to a station dealing with both through and terminating services plus, from February 1869, a branch service as well. At least an Up Platform Loop was provided after Colonel Yolland's Inspection of November 1866 in connection with the Braintree branch, when he described the place as 'not big enough' for the proposed services. By January 1869, workmen were engaged in enlarging the station and preparing a site for an engine turntable. This island platform was

a few yards south of the two platforms of 1845.

The island platform has never been really weatherproof with the prevailing westerly winds driving more rain under than on the meagre protecting awning which was authorised in November 1874. In 1885, this island platform was extended to allow a starting or terminating service to stand 'end to end' with the branch train. With development on the east side of the town an up side booking office was provided in 1895; this required an extension to the existing footbridge so that passengers from the London Road side could use all platforms.

Even with all this, the station was never really man enough to do the job expected of it. Down terminating trains had either to set back into the up sidings, pull forward into the back platform to run round or the engine had to run round first via the North Box then take its train across into the up sidings to propel into the back platform. Add to this the three through trains a day on the down line for Cambridge that recessed a while in the down siding for faster ones to pass or connect and you start to get the picture. Bishops Stortford South was a busy and interesting box to work but the frame 'pulled hard' and the signalman earned his corn. Just for good measure, the 'Loco Depot' such as it was, had no water column, all filling being done at the platform ends or in the goods yard, which all made for extra movements and could easily delay through services if not

As we approached the down side of the station for our train, this is what we would walk past. The condition of the area was long a bone of contention with the local Council and filling with crushed ballast from time to time by the GE was necessary. The goods shed of 1863 and office are in the background and the down side booking office and entrance is under the awning to the right. The parcels vans are an interesting mix; firstly there is the standard BR 'BG', followed in turn by a Thompson 'matchboard' BG, some of the longest vans built and five feet longer than the BR standard design. The slots for roofboards when in use on main line expresses are still there. This is followed by an LMS fish van, two vanfits and a BR standard insulated fish van. In the centre behind the shed is Edwards Mill in Dell Lane. It advertises 'Cattle, Pig and Poultry Foods' but was not rail connected. The large white building is the Falcon Hotel, starting point for 'Hicks Brothers' bus services to Dunmow and Braintree. There were twelve through journeys a day in February 1951 when in competition with the branch, fare 1/9d single. The cars are an interesting selection for connoisseurs, the one behind the 'No Parking' sign dating from November 1953.

carefully managed. With electrification in November 1960, down trains could at last run direct into either side of the 'up' side island and, better still, could get out again the other end. Nevertheless, the down side yard layout is, even today, still recognisable as it was in the 1950s apart from an aggregates

depit in the middle of it. The north end of the goods yard and shed has become the mandatory car park.

So let us turn back the clock and have a look at 'Bishops Stortford and beyond' before dieselisation.

The main station frontage before 'modernisation' struck. One semi-circular window has already been bricked up. The water tank for the station supply can be seen to the left; this is at the end of the siding at the Cambridge end, behind the down platform. The recognisable posters refer to cycle storage charges, football fares to Northumberland Park (for Tottenham Hotspur) and the Kursaal entertainment park at Southend. The low wooden building to the right is the telegraph office. Surely the Station Master never owned that car. On second thoughts, probably a Relief Signalman!

This must be 'pay day' in the booking hall with two locomen sorting their earnings and another waiting his turn at the Season Ticket window, apparently used as a paying out position on the appropriate day. Lots of activity here with a terminating train in the down platform being swept out, nicely showing a dropped window with a strap to raise it when finished, and a diligent ticket collector doing his job in a booth of the style of the time. The Bye Laws and 'Regulations for carrying traffic' are a mix of London & North Eastern Railway and BR. There is the statutory local OS Map in a frame and the platform ticket machine on the immediate left. Bicycles appear to be stored exactly where they landed when 'commuters' had left themselves just 30 seconds to get across the bridge to the up side.

Left. Most of the down platform seen from beneath the footbridge. 'Finlays for Tobacco, Cigarettes and Confectionery' is the first stall, followed by W.H. Smith. The 'Listener' leads with 'Russia, the atom and the West' and The Herts and Essex Observer is 'Your local paper'. There are various flat barrows on display and another (circular) water tank has sprung up. The engine siding at the far end was located behind the low wall next to the telegraph pole, which was another endangered species. The drifting smoke comes from the loco siding on the up side just off the right of the picture.

Bottom left. The down platform from the north end, taken from the loco siding. We can now see the culprit making the smoke nuisance, N7 0-6-2T 69687, a long standing Hertford engine. The adverts this end invite us to Bertram Mills Circus at Olympia and tell us 'There's no better job than a policeman's'. There is another (tender) engine tucked away in the Dock siding at the far end behind the 'Bishops Stortford' nameboard.

Below. It is 12 November 1959 and snow has come early this winter. A J20 0-6-0 is being prepared for a Braintree branch goods and the fireman trims the coal. The gas works, which was rail connected via a siding at the back of the goods yard, can be seen at the left-hand end of the tender and the Parish Church of St Michael's is seen in the mist above the station nameboard. The first (1842) station was roughly in the same direction just ahead of the J20. The locking bar may look odd on trailing points but this connection was used for passenger trains to set back into the down siding for expresses to pass. Sometimes they let passengers stay in, sometimes they turned you out. The fact that these trains ran over two further sets of unlocked points never crossed anyone's mind.

Left. The up island platform seen from the down side and looking south. The LNER 1930s South Box is just in view on the right. It is now one of only two such left on the GE lines. The hut under the bridge housed the auxiliary token instrument for the Dunmow/Braintree branch, being released by North Box with the Staff being handed to the driver by the Station Foreman. A coal train is pulling out at the far end. This view shows just how windswept this island platform could be.

Bottom left. Detail of the sparse buildings on the island platform – really just general and ladies waiting rooms, plus a W.H. Smiths which only opened for morning commuters. The 'Listener' for 5 December is a Christmas Book Number and the 'Radio Times' asks 'your opinion please'. Jersey and Broadstairs seek your attention and a six bay gents completes the scene.

Below. Britannia 70005 JOHN MILTON arrives at Bishops Stortford with an up local passenger in July 1955. 70005 came new to Stratford but had a spell at Rugby Testing Station in 1951 for 'performance and efficiency tests' being fitted with an exhaust steam injector. The train contains a Gresley 'Twin' set next to the engine. It looks like a Sunday by the number of engines 'on shed', at least three L1s and an N7 can be seen alongside the primitive coaling facilities. The Britannia, quite rightly, has at least two admirers on the down platform.

We move on northwards towards Stansted. This, as the chalked inscription on the right hand post tells us, is bridge 1492A, up side. Bridge 1492 replaced an Occupation Crossing with a gate hut and, as can be seen, needed to be upgraded by the 'A' version in this 1957 view. We are looking west with Bishops Stortford left and Stansted station right. The buffer stops are at the end of the down siding; the tall signal is Stansted Down Home No.20 which had high and low arms for sighting and a single Inner Distant (No.21) beneath the lower one. Near to this point, on the up side, once ran Rochford's tomato tramway. It consisted of a wagonway from the exchange sidings, up an incline, with wagons connected to an endless steel hawser, powered by a Paxton stationery steam engine. At the top, a small Ford vehicle shunted the miniature wagons around the glasshouses.

We are looking north through Stansted station; the double armed signals under the bridge are No.19 Down Main Starter and 17, Down Main to Down Loop. The covered footbridge, dating from the late 19th century, was replaced on electrification. The WHS bookstall is thought to date from 1931; it was demolished in 1985, but was closed some time before that.

Still looking north but a closer view showing some business in the coal siding beyond Church Road bridge (No.1494). The lamp room in front of the bridge was the first signal box here; built by A. Peck & Co of Cambridge in 1853, it lasted for about twenty years in that capacity. It survived until the demolition connected with electrification work in the 1980s. Mayhew's were 'garage owners and taxi proprietors'. They operated the first taxi cabs in the village. The station gardens, which won many prizes, are seen to advantage.

Still 1957 and looking south through Church Road bridge. The short platforms which held only five coaches on the up and four on the down created some problems, particularly with down trains 'drawing up' which then lost the driver's vision due to the intervening bridge. Minutes could easily be lost here trying to convey hand and lamp signals. The line on the extreme right is the south end of the short coal siding.

Left. Onward again to Elsenham, (and change for Thaxted between 1913 and 1952). We are looking west from the window of a Thaxted-bound train as it leaves the branch platform on 30 June 1951. The station nameboard advises us that it is 'Elsenham for Thaxted Line'. The signal box is the third here, all being almost in the same place. This one dates from 1932 and is an LNER Type 11A example with 45 levers, which came into use when a Down Loop and Two Up Loops were provided. It lasted until 11 December 1983, when it was absorbed in the Cambridge Power Box scheme. Photograph H.C. Casserley.

Bottom left. Austerity 90393 passes the oil lit station with an up Class 'F' in the early 1950s. As late as summer 1952, there were 36 up freights in a weekday 24 hours through Elsenham. Elsenham was another place with a long record of 'Best Kept Station' awards, latterly under Station Master Sell before Area Managers took over. 90393 went to Immingham in October 1953 when March had a 'K3 invasion' in one of the many block changes of power we had over the years.

Below. A brief look at Newport (Essex) on 11 May 1960 as B1 61252 arrives with the 7.16am Cambridge-Liverpool Street. The footbridge was damaged beyond repair when a railborne crane collided with it two months later. The porters' room this side of the bridge on the down platform became the signal box between 11 November 1972 and 11 December 1983 after the 'real thing' was demolished in an accident. The 7.16 from Cambridge called at all stations to Bishops Stortford then Burnt Mill, already reflecting the importance of Harlow New Town and Liverpool Street. It will be noted that the train is non-corridor stock. 61252 itself was a long-standing Ipswich engine; pushed out by dieselisation there, it came to Cambridge in January 1960. Photograph B. Wilson, The Transport Treasury.

Final destination, Audley end. Firstly, the south end at the main line junction for the Saffron Walden branch. Seen from the signal box steps, B17 4-6-0 61626, BRANCEPETH CASTLE of March shed comes off the viaduct with the 1.24pm Liverpool Street to Cambridge on Saturday 25 July 1959. This train called at Broxbourne, where it shed an all-stations portion for Bishops Stortford, then ran fast to that point itself and all-stations to Cambridge. Photograph B. Wilson, The Transport Treasury.

Still at the south end, B1 4-6-0 61283 departs with the 1.15pm Cambridge-Liverpool Street express on 15 October 1960. To the right of the train the lines lead to firstly the dock siding and Barnard Bros. granary, then to the down branch platform and from the up branch loop. The spur in the foreground was used in the days when the branch loco had to run round every trip, before push and pull working began in July 1951. Note the old carriage for Signal & Telegraph staff on right. Photograph B. Wilson, The Transport Treasury.

The station itself, looking north. Beyond the bridge are the up passenger and down goods loops. To the right is the goods shed, once served by two wagon turntables of which one can still be seen just behind the right-hand legs of the footbridge.

The procession of freight trains on the Cambridge line was never-ending. Here we have O1 2-8-0 63650 passing the down platform with a Whitemoor-Temple Mills Class 'H' on 4 April 1959. The train has a rarely photographed 'Boplate' wagon behind the tender. The loco, still with oval buffers, has been cleaned. That says something for the dedication of March shed, especially with dieselisation breaking out all around them. In another one of the 'class transfers' in spring 1957, a batch of O1s came from Annesley to push out more WDs. Photograph B. Wilson, The Transport Treasury.

Holiday Fourum Camping Coach Contrasts
Andrew McRae

Crianlarich in 1939, with K4 2-6-0 No 3445 MacCAILIN MOR on a Glasgow train. The venerable MSLR six wheeler ahead of it has already seen several years service as a camping coach, the LNER having been the initiators of the concept in 1933.

Gleaming wood panelling on the Southern in 1936; a hint that the SR sought to distinguish its holiday coaches as 'luxury camps'. This is one of six former LSW lavatory composites that became 'campers' Nos.13-18. The fencing visible through the drop-light is rather untypical of such publicity shots; usually the scene was some rural idyll, 'cut and pasted' into the window area to hide a mundane corner of a workshop yard.

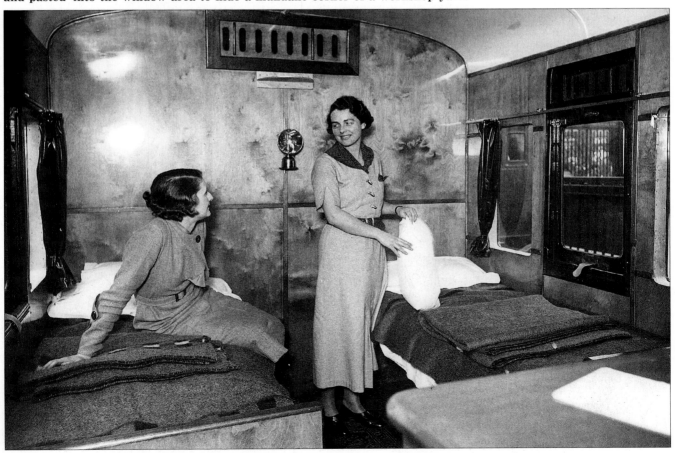

Abergele July 1959. This picture has been published before but surely deserves a second outing, encapsulating as it does the very essence of a camping coach holiday and the innocence of the age. Shades of those old school photos; but all is accomplished with a charming air of informality, the subjects squinting awkwardly in the bright morning sunshine.

Aberdovey in 1964, with the humble camping coach illustrating the regional boundary changes implemented in January 1963 under which the Cambrian coast lines switched from Western to LMR control. Whereas W9924W retains its historic colours of chocolate and cream, its neighbour W9928W has evidently paid a visit to works during the winter for a repaint in its new owner's camping livery of green and cream. Western 'purists' were no doubt aghast at such a development but worse was to follow, as the LM operating authorities evidently didn't think much of this inherited stock. The vehicles were scrapped at the end of 1964 and replaced the following season by ex-LNW coaches. Andrew McRae was responsible for the elegiac tribute to what must be a uniquely British holiday institution, the Camping Coach in *British Railways Camping Coach Holidays* Parts 1 and 2 (Foxline Publishing) and various items and reviews have appeared in BRILL in recent years.

The Last 4-4-0 Expresses

A Footplate Pass with R.C. Riley, 14 May 1960

By 1960 there was no service left in the country that could be said to be fast (of a sort) and regular over a decent distance that was entrusted to inside cylinder 4-4-0s. Except one, from Holborn Viaduct and London Bridge to the Kent Coast. It couldn't last and 1960, in fact, was the final full year of these workings. On summer Saturdays in particular several 4-4-0s of the two or three surviving classes (D1, E1, L and L1) might be observed. It might not sound much, but this was already a more or less vanished spectacle, the very last relic of the sort of train working that had been ubiquitous in Britain over many decades. Top, on Saturday 14 May 1960, D1 31489 is ready to leave London Bridge while below we are out on the road, at Hither Green. Photographs R.C. Riley, The Transport Treasury.

Above, 31489 approaches Grove Park; below, the train is nearing Elmstead Tunnels. The working was the 7.24am London Bridge to Ramsgate, on the 'long way round' via Tonbridge, Ashford and Folkestone, first stop Orpington. The train was made up of five corridors and three vans, to 198 tons and actually started from Holborn Viaduct, which was an important parcels handling station back then. The train ran without passengers from there and only became a passenger train proper at London Bridge. An historical curiosity is that a fox and cubs were observed near the Elmstead Tunnels. Nothing out of the ordinary in that, one might think, but back then it prompted a letter to The Times, for it was the nearest to the capital that foxes had then been observed! Photographs R.C. Riley, The Transport Treasury.

The Way Ahead 1. Top, 31489 is about to call at Orpington and, below, is leaving Sevenoaks. The train had left London Bridge a minute late; Sevenoaks was the first stop, where it was 'on time'. Photographs R.C. Riley, The Transport Treasury.

The Way Ahead 2. Top, 31489 near Tonbridge and, below, leaving. Time was starting to slip now and arrival at Tonbridge had been four minutes late, due to heavy PW slacks south of Hildenborough. The D1 had to take water at Tonbridge but quick work saw 31489 away only three minutes late. Photographs R.C. Riley, The Transport Treasury.

Arrival at Ashford (top) and, below, at Folkestone Junction. Three vans were added at Ashford, where arrival had been four minutes late, and the train was 're-timed' (it should have left at 9am) to 9.06 to let a 'non-parcels' train pass forward. This was a somewhat daunting excursion from Portsmouth (where it had left at the ungodly time of 5.52am) to Folkestone; an incomprehensible trip (who would do that nowadays?) to us now, it was due at Folkestone at 9.15am. Photographs R.C. Riley, The Transport Treasury.

Final view from the footplate, at Folkestone Junction. The train was now more than ten minutes late despite the re-timing and in the end, by the time it got to Dover, the deficit was fourteen minutes, made worse by the need to detach three vans and delays to unloading the others. Our 7.24am became a stopper onwards from Dover, calling at Martin Mill, Walmer, Deal and Sandwich, to arrive twenty-five minutes late at Ramsgate, at 10.59am. The Inspector explained that the delay was due to engineering work, extra loading and unloading of mail and an inexperienced fireman. The engine itself was in excellent condition, having passed through works in January, a few months before. A vagary of civil engineering on the Southern (coupled no doubt to the knowledge that electrification was in the offing) meant that Pacifics were too heavy for the many bridges and structures among the London streets between Holborn Viaduct and London Bridge. There was no arrangement for changing engines at London Bridge so the 4-4-0s continued on the trains for an unlikely service survival. Electrification finally ended this English 4-4-0 swansong the following year. Photographs R.C. Riley, The Transport Treasury.

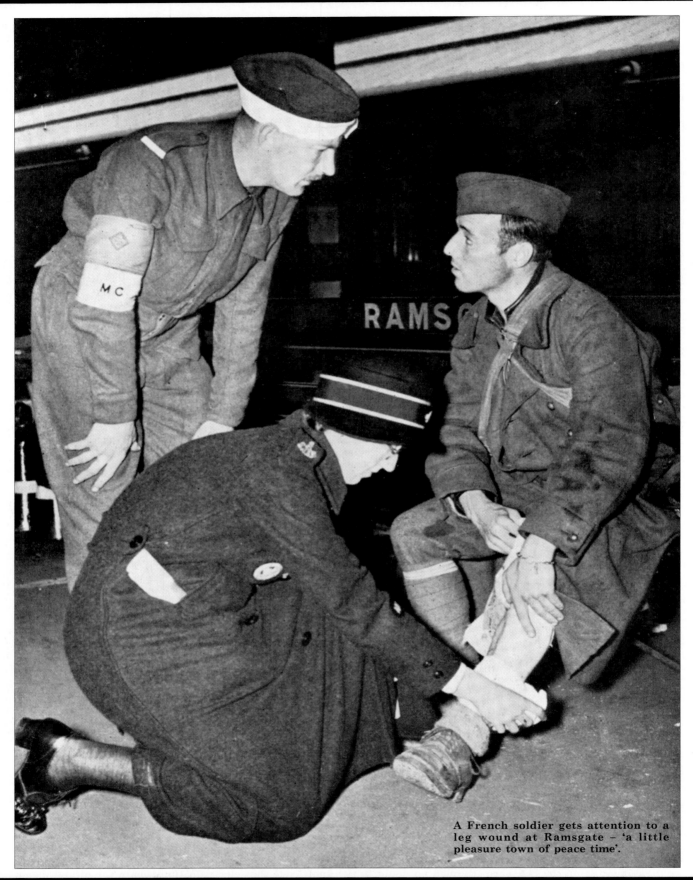

A French soldier gets attention to a
leg wound at Ramsgate – 'a little
pleasure town of peace time'.

The first part of the journey back through the peaceful Kent countryside must have been a relief beyond measure. Special stops were organised for tea and sandwiches and children and adults gathered to cheer the trains.

HOME FROM DUNKIRK

The Social Railway: Some Thoughts on Railway Life
Roger Hockney

Many books have been written about our railways. Even more pamphlets and articles have appeared over the years. Almost all concentrate on technical subjects, or railway history. Occasionally, someone holds the torch for railway architecture. Hardly ever do we come across an article about the social activities of railway workers. Perhaps it was because of the difficult hours; perhaps because many were often on the move to new places of work and so new relationships outside of work were difficult to establish, but for whatever reason, the railway community was tight and often inward looking, working and playing together. We can glean much about the way of life of the railway community by looking at the post war Railwaymen's Year Books. Not surprisingly, they are also a microcosm of the British way of life at the end of the Second World War. The first covers 1946/47. The second edition in 1947/48 tells us that the editors *shall not be satisfied with our efforts until we have achieved our aim of a complete and comprehensive Year Book for the use of railway workers of all grades.* And this indeed was the case. A glance at the contents pages gives us a flavour of the range of information in the book. Everything from (predictably) new railway developments, to the promotion of convalescent homes, allotment competitions and advice on national insurance tables can be found within its pages, to be replicated and updated in subsequent issues.

Predictably, the books have a heavy emphasis on trade unionism. In 1947, the Railway Clerks' Association had a membership of 90,000; ASLEF 74,000 and the NUR 260,000. The structure of trade union negotiation on the railway was well developed and railway trade union leaders often could be found on local councils as well as serving in Parliament. Pictures of the thirty railway MPs, all with studied looks of seriousness, fill a couple of early pages. Then there's the list of railwaymen who were in distinguished positions in HM Government. We often forget that the ethic of public service translated easily to government service as well as running railways. But what about the day to day social organisations and events fostered or supported by the railway companies? Here's a brief dip into them.

In 1947, over 9,000 horses worked for the railways. Using the LMS as an example, to quote the Year Book: *Quite apart from purely domestic events, 350 carters from 70 stations entered their horses in public shows during 1946, and secured 34 First, 45 Second and 39 Third class awards, beside 7 cups and 99 other prizes..... The carters- even after a hard day's work- stay long into the night cleaning, brushing ,burnishing, plaiting and polishing so that their precious charges will look their best when the great day dawns.* Railway horse shows were great crowd draws. In 1946, nearly 3,000 spectators attended the LMS International Horse Parade in Glasgow: *It would prove a sorry day if such customs were allowed to die out and even more regrettable should the only substitute be an array of inanimate motor vehicles.*

1946 saw the opening of the ninth railway convalescent home, at Buxton. *This new home has raised the* standard still higher by providing hot and cold water in every bedroom and in most cases the patient has a room to himself. Three homes were available for women and *the babies are kept quite apart from other patients and special nurses are provided to look after them.* But such were the burdens placed on the trustees, what with the increases in the prices of coal and electricity, that they announced that the railway workers' subscriptions would have to be increased from a halfpenny a week to a penny. Despite this increase, readers of the book are encouraged to sign up: *It is too late to wait until overtaken by sickness; the wise railwayman or woman will join now.* We have to remember that in 1947, the National Health Service did not exist and to work for an organisation that provided such facilities underlines the railways' forward looking commitment to staff welfare.

The reader will note that the book is the Railwaymen's Year Book and that there appears to be a distinct lack

				whole of	
				July 7th, 1947.	
					9s. 0d.
age(s) of					
		1st £50, 3s. 0d.		Next £75, 6s. 0d.	
			Remainder 9s. 0d.		
earned income allowance			One-sixth		

Personal allowances :—

Single person	£110	Married couple	£180
Married woman in industry	£110	Child	£60

The following tables give examples of total income tax payable on earned income during the year 1947-1948, after deduction of personal allowances, married allowances, child allowances, and earned income relief. The taxpayer may be entitled to further reliefs (*e.g.*, on life assurance premiums or N.H.I. contributions) which would reduce the tax payable below the amounts shewn.

Single Persons

Income Per annum £	Per week s.	d.	Tax payable £	s.	d.
140	54	0	1	0	0
150	57	6	2	5	0
160	61	6	3	10	0
170	65	6	4	15	0
200	77	0	9	10	0
225	86	6	15	15	0
250	96	0	22	0	0
300	115	6	36	15	0
320	122	6	44	5	0
350	134	6	55	10	0

Married Couple no children

225	86	6	1	0	0
250	96	0	4	5	0
300	115	6	13	10	0
320	122	6	18	10	0
350	134	6	26	0	0
400	154	0	42	15	0
500	192	0	80	5	0
600	231	0	117	15	0

Married Couple One child

Income Per annum £	Per week s.	d.	Tax payable £	s.	d.
300	115	6	1	0	0
320	122	6	4	0	0
350	134	6	8	0	0
400	154	0	20	0	0
500	192	0	53	0	0
600	231	0	90	0	0

Married Couple Two children

350	134	6	Nil		
375	144	6	2	0	0
400	154	0	5	0	0
500	192	0	27	0	0
600	231	0	63	0	0

Married Couple Three children

425	163	6	Nil		
450	173	0	2	0	0
500	192	0	9	0	0
600	231	0	37	0	0

(Tax figures rounded off to nearest 5s. 0d.)

of political correctness in the air. There is, however, a whole section in the 1946/47 edition on Railway Women. Inevitably, after the Second World War during which women took over many jobs hitherto occupied by

CRACK TRAINS of BRITAIN

SOUTHERN RAILWAY

AFTER a lapse of over six years the Southern Railway, on 15th April 1946, restored the famous " Golden Arrow " service between London and Paris, via Dover and Calais. With its seven first and second class Pullman cars and " Trianon Bar " car, the " Golden Arrow " is one of the world's most luxurious trains. It is fitted throughout with loud-speaker equipment.

On its daily schedule, the " Golden Arrow " leaves London (Victoria) at 10.0 a.m., connects with steamer at Dover which links up with the train's counterpart at Calais providing for an arrival in Paris by 6.45 p.m. The return service leaves Paris at 11.35 a.m. and arrives at Victoria 8.35 p.m.

When Mr. Alfred Barnes, Minister of Transport, attended the re-opening of the " Golden Arrow " service at Victoria, he said the occasion was of special significance in the opportunity it gave of renewing contacts with France, of the importance of whose civilisation the war had given us a deeper realisation.

By courtesy of S.R.]
The Southern Railway's " Golden Arrow " at speed. During May 1947 the service was speeded up, departure from Paris being timed 12 noon and arrival at London (Victoria) 8-40 p.m.

Also after an interval of seven years, the Southern Railway's famous express " Bournemouth Belle," comprised of ten Pullman cars, weighing 400 tons approximately, with full dining car facilities, and loud-speaker installation, resumed public service on 7th October 1946.

53

obligatory best kept station competitions, the companies supported federations of railway horticultural societies, which often occupied railway owned land. There were nearly 80,000 lineside plots on 4,100 acres of land immediately after the war. It's surprising that photographs don't show that many lineside allotments, since so much land was set aside for that use. *Over 10,000 railway workers are members of the LMS Federation of Horticultural Societies and in a recent year they purchased 240 tons of seed potatoes, 230 tons of fertilisers and £1,000 worth of small seeds.* The Year Books also sought to keep railway gardeners apprised of new horticultural developments, as well as providing advice on the gardening year. Three railway companies revived best kept station competitions immediately after the war, whilst the Southern Railway chose to rely on individual efforts at stations. It should also be remembered that the competitions were not just about gardening. On the LMS *marks will be awarded for cultivation of flowers and shrubs; general cleanliness of the station, waiting rooms and offices and for neatness in display of posters, etc.* It was stressed that urban stations had just as much chance of winning as rural stations. The latter had not suffered the trials of the war to such an extent as urban stations.

The British Railways Staff Association, was founded in 1952. Its aims were *to develop social and recreative activities amongst British Railways staff and their families; to foster the spirit of fellowship and goodwill and to do everything possible to further the prestige of British Railways.* It arose because of the realisation that the pre-nationalisation companies had

men, there's a healthy recognition of the importance of women in building the post war railway. At the end of the war nearly 60,000 women worked for the railway companies and London Transport, down from a 1943 peak of 93,000. All railway companies created women's welfare organisations *to provide suitable amenities to meet the influx of women workers.*

No account of social events would be complete without considering gardening. Such is its importance that it takes up nearly four pages in the 1947/48 Year Book. Besides the

Diesels Come to Britain. It is significant in the light of fuel problems on British railways to observe the latest move of the London, Midland & Scottish Railway, in the matter of adopting diesel-electric traction for main-line services.

The first experimental design is for a diesel-electric locomotive of 3,200 h.p. (composed of two 1,600 h.p. units) which will be capable of working services comparable with the pre-war Coronation Scot train, normally worked by the L.M.S. 4-6-2 steam locomotives of world fame. The weight of the new diesels will be 220 tons and speeds of 100 miles an hour will be possible on favourable track.

These main-line diesel-electric locomotives will result in a substantial saving of coal; for example, a main-line unit of 3,200 h.p. would on its annual mileage save some 2,500 tons of coal fuel per year.

Great Britain has a long way to go before it reaches the standard set in the United States of America in diesel propulsion. Details are now to hand of a new 8,000 h.p. diesel-electric locomotive which has been placed into service there, but, of course, conditions in the two countries are vastly different from the fuel angle, and although for the present we find it necessary to adopt alternatives, coal will prove to be the main factor in this country eventually.

PROGRESSIVE PLANS OF BRITISH RAILWAYS

IN keeping with our policy to provide information regarding schemes framed to improve the railways of this country, we sought detail from the new Railway Executive, London Transport Executive and the Regional Officers for inclusion in this issue.

The response clearly indicated that the high degree of enterprise and initiative, for which the former private railway companies were world-famed, has not diminished because of transfer to State ownership. In fact, realising our space limitations, we were embarrassed by the volume of material which was immediately placed at our disposal.

Whilst admitting inability to do justice to the subject, we are pleased to be able to supply the following abridged versions of the more important schemes, together with some interesting illustrations, and trust in a future issue there will be an opportunity to provide more space for these important matters.

Many of the schemes, of course, were launched just before the private railway companies ceased to exist.

LONDON MIDLAND REGION

An important landmark in the history of locomotive development was reached on December 27, 1947, when the first diesel-electric locomotive to be constructed for experimental main line service in Great Britain was completed at the L.M.S. Works at Derby.

This first locomotive is powered by a 16-cylinder 1,600 h.p. " English Electric " diesel engine, which, together with the whole of the control equipment, has been designed and manufactured by The English Electric

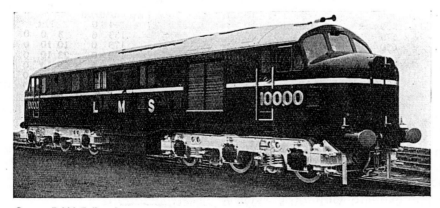

Courtesy British Railways]
L.M.S. Main Line Diesel Electric Locomotive No. 10,000

supported the establishment of many off duty activities; sports, hobbies, music and art, horticulture and crafts, for example. Although membership was described as voluntary, members had to pay four pence a week by 1956. It was more than just a vehicle for running social events, but was seen as a 'rallying point' for the many thousands of railway staff and their dependants who desired 'opportunities for self expression'.

The Railway Mission is also still with us. It arose as a consequence of concern over the welfare of young boys working for the railways in South London. In the last quarter of the nineteenth century it is estimated that about 17,000 lads worked for the railways in London alone. Bible classes were started for them, often held in waiting rooms. As the movement gathered momentum, it was formally established as the Railway Mission in 1881, with branches set up across the country. In 1947, there were 80 branches.

Staff welfare on a wider basis was provided through the Joint Advisory Council for Staff Welfare, set up after nationalisation *for the purpose of promoting and encouraging measures affecting the safety ,health and welfare of railway staff.* The 1956 Year Book tells us that *within the last four and a half years nearly seven and a half million pounds have been authorised for the provision of improved staff amenities, including lavatories, messrooms, drinking water supplies, lockers, cloakrooms, facilities for the drying of clothing, rest rooms, hostels, first aid accommodation, canteens, lengthmen's huts, heating, ventilation and lighting.* Then there were the railway training schools. No less than five pages of the !947/48 Year Book are dedicated to a description of the training courses available in house for staff. These range from the LMS School of Transport at Derby and the SR Staff Training College at Woking for senior managers, down to the Primary Training Centre at Scarborough (available to female staff) which trained staff on goods and passenger station accounts and the SR Staff Typing School at London Bridge (female staff only).

As the nation recovered from the war, thoughts once again turned to holidays. The Year Books gave advice to the holidaymaker on where to go and what to enjoy at those destinations. First there was the getting there. The Railway Employees' Privilege Ticket Association sought to reassure staff that nationalisation would not affect their opportunity to use free passes and privilege tickets. Indeed, discounts for members extended beyond railway use to, for example, the zoos at Regents Park, Whipsnade, Edinburgh and Dudley. *At the Royal Pavilion, Brighton, production of the membership card gains entrance at half price; at Southend's Kursaal Amusement Centre the magic card takes its owner in free, and away north at Dunoon a ten per cent reduction is allowed on the* *Fitzpatrick Blue Motor Coach Tours. These are but a few of the numerous examples chosen from lists which bid fair to attain pre war proportions before long.*

There are tips as to which resorts to go to; Ramsgate, with its *brilliant record for sunshine,* Brighton is *almost as bright as it was in the good old days* and Eastbourne is *fast gaining in popularity.* And of course the Books put in a good word for holiday camps: *Those who regularly use these camps would never dream of an alternative, and those who taste a camp for the first time may be heard to say, "Only such for me in the future".*

This has been a brief exploration of that extensive infrastructure of social activities which underpinned railway society. We have not even touched on the importance of Mutual Improvement Classes, which provided a form of self help education which stands as a precursor of today's direct learning; fire-fighting competitions; the Railway Benevolent In-stitution; first aid classes and railway choirs. Whilst some activities still continue today, many have simply disappeared with the emergence of a much wider choice of leisure and recreation activities. As income has risen, along with increased choice, so the need to make one's own enter-tainment locally has significantly reduced, but we should not underestimate the important and forward looking role that the railway companies played in supporting their staffs' social activities.

RAILWAYMEN'S GARDENS

In keeping with our aim to provide readers of this Year Book *with the best guidance obtainable we commissioned Mr. Geo. H. Copley to write special articles for this section and to provide separate gardening calendars covering the cultivation of fruit, flowers and vegetables. These contributions —which are strictly copyright—appear on the ensuing pages.*

Mr. Geo. H. Copley, N.D.H., the author of our Gardening Section, is the elder son of Mr. Frederick Copley, a well-known Yorkshire gardener, who for many years was Superintendent of Parks at Mirfield.

Mr. G. H. Copley has held important educational and administrative appointments in horticulture. He is now widely known as gardening adviser, lecturer, writer of books and articles and as a broadcaster.

In the picture he is examining compost with Miss Maye E. Bruce, who is probably the world's greatest authority on compost and composting.

79

Hurrying home. 'Empties to Colliery' north of Standish Junction behind 0-8-0 49154, 7 September 1960.